A WESLEYAN SPIRITUAL READER

A WESLEYAN SPIRITUAL READER

❖

Rueben P. Job

ABINGDON PRESS
Nashville

A WESLEYAN SPIRITUAL READER

Copyright © 1998 by Abingdon Press

All rights reserved.

This book is printed on recycled, acid-free paper.

——— *Book design by J.S.Lofbomm* ———

Library of Congress Cataloging-in-Publication Data

Job, Rueben P.
  A Wesleyan Spiritual Reader / Rueben P. Job
    p. cm.
  Includes bibliographical references and index.
  ISBN 0-687-05701-9 (pbk.   : alk. paper)
  1. Devotional calendars.   2. Spiritual life—Christianity.   3. Christian life—Methodist authors.   I. Title.
BV4811.J56   1998
242'.2—dc21   98-38332
                                                                                CIP

All scripture quotations original to this work are from the New Revised Standard Version of the Bible, copyright © 1989 by the Division of Christian Education of the National Council of Churches of Christ in the USA. Used by permission.

The original letters of John Wesley shown on the cover were pho-tographed with permission of The Upper Room Museum, Nashville, Tennessee.

98 99 00 01 02 03 04 05 06 10 9 8 7 6 5 4 3 2

MANUFACTURED IN THE UNITED STATES OF AMERICA

*For our children
and their families,
Deborah
Ann
Philip
David
whose lives continue
to reveal God's grace.*

CONTENTS

❖

INTRODUCTION

John Wesley has been rediscovered! This rediscovery has resulted in numerous publications reflecting his enormous contribution to the Christian faith in general and Methodism in particular. This book is intended as a spiritual reader that gives a taste of Wesley's thought and spirit. Each week's reading includes excerpts from Wesley's writing around a particular theme. Scripture readings and contemporary reflection on each theme provide the content for a daily time of prayer and reflection. While these selections do not adequately cover the immense scope of Wesley's thought or writing, they do make original material available for the contemporary reader. The twenty-six themes addressed here are not exhaustive but illustrative of the wisdom and insight provided by the founder of the Methodist movement.

What is gathered here is an introduction to the mind and heart of one of the significant spiritual leaders of the Christian faith. The material is best approached as *spiritual reading*, permitting the reader to listen for and hear God's voice in the contents of daily readings and to see their application to the everyday experiences of life. John Wesley was convinced that holiness is discovered in the practice of our faith in the practical and everyday routines of life. Therefore he fashioned for himself a way of living that included time for reading and reflecting upon scripture and other spiritual works and methods for putting into practice what he believed and what he heard God calling him to do.

Spiritual reading is a new discovery for many Protestants. There is an increasing hunger for resources that can offer spiritual guidance. While spiritual reading can never replace a spiritual director, spiritual friend, or spiritual community, it is a practice that can tie our separate lives to the larger community of faith and, ultimately, to God.

Through spiritual reading we can become connected to the saints who have gone before us. They can become for us companions on our journey and we can learn from them, be guided and directed by their experience and witness. Their voices can address our lives with insight and wisdom gained by faithful living and tested by centuries of examination and practice.

Through spiritual reading we can also become connected to and companions with our contemporaries who are discovering helpful insights into our shared journey towards God. They are familiar with our contemporary world but bring wisdom gained in disciplined search, as they have listened and responded to God's gracious initiative to be our companion in life and death.

These companions from many generations can introduce us again and again to the One all Christians seek to follow. Their wisdom, gained from their own efforts to live in faithfulness, can often give us insight, encouragement and direction. Spiritual reading can put us in touch with the great spiritual directors of all time.

Trying to travel the spiritual path alone is foolish, risky, and will ultimately end in failure. Spiritual reading makes that lonely journey unnecessary. Many find that such reading is done best in connection with a time of prayer and reflection.

How Shall I Begin?

Set aside a time for attention to your relationship with God. This can be early or late, whatever suits your needs. Many find early morning hours most fruitful and helpful preparation for the day. But each of us is unique, so find the time that works best for you. If this is a new practice for you, begin modestly. Try ten or fifteen minutes and then move on until you can commit and benefit from an hour or more of time in discovering, enjoying, and nurturing your relationship with God.

Daily Pattern. The suggested liturgy for each day includes scripture reading, silence, spiritual reading, recording (journal writing), prayer, reflection on a hymn portion, offering your life to God, and a closing affirmation. While you will want to adapt the liturgy to meet your own spiritual needs, and the time available, it is important to establish a pattern and then to follow it regularly. You will reap rich rewards from a disciplined approach to your spiritual life.

Scripture Reading. The Bible is unique in its capacity to

convey the message of God in every age and circumstance. Those who read daily from the Bible and reflect upon its meaning are gradually formed more and more into the image of the God who is portrayed and revealed in this sacred book. Regular reading and reflecting upon the scriptures has a profound effect upon us. Over time we begin to think like God, and even to act like God. Reading and reflection upon scripture is an important step along the path that leads to holiness. The asterisk beside one of the seven scriptures listed each week identifies the passage recommended to those preaching or teaching on that theme.

Silence. Silence has been highly valued as a spiritual discipline within the monastic community. There is good reason. God speaks to us in sound and silence, and yet our noisy world often crowds out the voice of God that comes in silence. Take a few moments to sit quietly and just listen. Do not be alarmed at the voices you hear within. Excuse yourself from the presence of those inner and outer voices and gently lead yourself back to silence. Today, speak less and listen more. Tonight, before you enter the silence of sleep, review your experience of silence and its contribution to listening for the voice of God during the day about to close.

Spiritual Reading. You may wish to read the reflections on each theme early in the week, then sample the Wesley quotes and the contemporary response to the theme (where included). While the book is set up for a week's reading, feel free to modify this to meet your own needs. There is enough content in each week's design to provide more than enough material for a month of reflection. Do not hesitate to experiment until you find the most fruitful way to use this resource for your own spiritual nurture and growth.

While there are approximately the same number of pages devoted to the Spiritual Reading for each week, the selections do not follow a rigid pattern. For some themes, a contemporary commentator is included, while for others, John Wesley is the sole source. In most weeks, there is a variety of brief quotations, but occasionally one or two longer quotations seemed to provide the best help to readers in furthering their own reflection of the topic.

John Wesley's quotations are taken from *The Works of John Wesley* edited by Thomas Jackson in 1831. In preparing this manuscript, I have been greatly assisted by *The Works of John Wesley on Compact Disc* (Franklin, TN: Providence House Publishers) which provides helpful access to the fourteen volume Jackson edition.

The quotations of John Wesley are presented in their original form. Wesley lived in an era when the use of "man" to represent humankind was the standard convention. It is my hope that all readers, men and women, will "read past" this language and absorb the wisdom and passion John Wesley still offers us today.

Recording Insights. Many people find that recording thoughts and questions is a wonderful way of capturing and preserving the insights of the moment. This record or journal can also yield rich fruit as you periodically go over what you have written. As you read what you have recorded, I think you will find John Wesley speaking to you through your own words as well as through his.

Prayer. Prayer is both gift and treasure that must be practiced if it is to be learned and incorporated into the fabric of everyday life. Many find that the psalms and the prayers of ancient and contemporary spiritual leaders serve to teach and encourage their own life of prayer. We may think of prayer as stating our needs before God—and this is an important element of prayer. But it is a definition far too small. Prayer is a revolutionary act and may lead us where we did not expect to go and shape us in ways we had not anticipated. Prayer is not only a crying out for God's help, it is not only an invitation for God to intervene in our lives, it is also an offering up of all that we are, have, and hope to become to the One who loves us.

Hymn Portion. Charles Wesley was one of the most prolific and gifted hymn writers of the Christian church. His contribution of poetry to his time and to ours is enormous. His poetry shaped and taught the theology of the early Methodist movement. It was a poetry and theology that was accessible to the common person. It moved and shaped the Methodist movement in its beginnings and can do the same for us. Try to commit the week's hymn portion to memory so that you can reflect upon it throughout the day. Unless otherwise noted, the references given are to *The United Methodist Hymnal* (UMH).

Offering All of Life to God. All times of prayer include an offering of self. However, as we conclude this time of intimate sharing and communion with God, and as we remember who we are as creatures of the loving Creator, an offering of self to God in faith and obedience is a natural and appropriate response. This is a time to place your life, those you love, and your concerns, joys, hopes, and activities for the day into the hands of God. To do so is to find strength, courage, and assurance.

Closing Affirmation. There is real and strong temptation to permit our fears and doubts to guide and shape our lives. By living with an affirmation, we render helpless and harmless the fears and doubts that so often overtake us.

You may find it helpful to place the opening scripture sentence and the closing affirmation on a card for your desk, mirror, or refrigerator door—wherever you are most likely to see it throughout the day. This is another way to help us remember that all of life is lived out under the loving gaze of God and that our relationship with God can be recognized and nurtured all day long and in every circumstance.

Welcome to *A Wesleyan Spiritual Reader.* My hope is that it will be a point of beginning for those who are considering a serious commitment to their life in the Spirit as well as for those who have been on this journey for a long time. In a letter to John Trembath, John Wesley said:

> O begin! Fix some part of every day for private exercises. You may acquire the taste for which you have not: What is tedious at first will afterwards be pleasant. Whether you like it or no, read and pray daily. It is for your life: there is no other way... Do justice to your own soul: give it time and means to grow. Do not starve yourself any longer. Take up your cross and be a Christian altogether. Then will the children of God rejoice.

Let us accept his words as a letter to us and begin today, for the first time or as a continuation of our desire, to "do justice to [our] own soul."

1

Living Prayerfully

❖— *Scripture Sentence*
> He was praying in a certain place, and after he had
> finished, one of his disciples said to him,"Lord, teach
> us to pray." *Luke 11:1*

❖— *Scripture Readings*

*Luke 11:2-13	Acts 4:23-31
Luke 18:1-14	Romans 12:9-21
John 17:6-19	1 Thessalonians 3:6-13
John 17:20-26	

❖— *Silence for Meditation*

❖— *Spiritual Reading*

❖— *Recording Insights and Commitments*

❖— *Prayers of Thanks, Intercession, Petition, and Praise*

❖— *Hymn Portion*
> Pray without ceasing, pray, (your Captain gives the
> word) his summons cheerfully obey and call upon
> the Lord; to God your every want in instant prayer
> display, pray always, pray and never faint, pray,
> without ceasing pray. *UMH #513*

❖— *Offering All of Life to God*

❖— *Closing Affirmation*
> The prayer of faith will save the sick, and the Lord
> will raise them up; and anyone who has committed
> sins will be forgiven. . . . The prayer of the righteous
> is powerful and effective. *James 5:15-16*

Asterisk indicates text recommended for preaching and teaching.

———— *Reflections* ————

Most of us have a strong desire to deepen and strengthen our sense of living with God in the daily activities of life. In our better moments we want a more intimate relationship with God. We really do want to experience God's companionship in all of life because we know that life is incomplete without this central experience of God. We want to claim and to enjoy our full inheritance as children of God. And yet, more often than not our desires are snuffed out in their infancy, and we are captured by the pressures, enticements, and false rewards of our culture.

John Wesley saw and experienced what we see and experience. It is impossible to live as a Christian if we are unattached to God. Our spiritual and even our physical lives become a shambles without the constant companionship with God that prayer alone can make possible. Consequently, Wesley determined to be a man of ardent and consistent prayer. An exact replica of his disciplined life of prayer may not be possible for us, but it can be instructive as we fashion our own way of living with God in the world.

Wesley knew that a life of prayer was not an accident or a natural consequence of just living. He was convinced that a life of prayer was the result of a determined and disciplined effort. He knew from personal experience that without this disciplined effort, prayer would become secondary and our relationship with God left to suffocate under the cares and delights of the world. So, the disciplined life of prayer became a priority that he honored for his entire lifetime.

Even a casual acquaintance with his journal will reveal that this disciplined life of prayer did not diminish his commitment to or involvement with the world of everyday cares and affairs. As a matter of fact, it seems clear that his involvement in the affairs of life received direction and power from the priority given to prayer.

John Wesley taught and lived a life of private, public, family, and community prayer. His earliest publishing venture was to provide direction and example for the person seeking to live a life of prayer. Prayers for families, children, clergy, the poor, prisoners, the sick, governmental and ecclesiastical authority, and prayers for self are found throughout his journal and sermons. Prayer was integral to his life.

When we read Wesley's journal and reflect upon his disciplined life, we can easily be convinced that such a life of prayer is impossible in our time and in our situation. Life is more complex and is changing more rapidly now than in the eighteenth century. The pressures on our time and life are different and more varied than the pressures John Wesley experienced. On the other hand, this kind of reflection on Wesley's life makes it clear that he often lived in a time squeeze and felt himself to be in a pressure cooker just as we do. Looking back over two centuries it is easy to see that this pressure cooker was, for the most part, self imposed and fueled by his sense of mission. He was able to live creatively within this pressure because he continued a disciplined life of prayer.

Prayer is a natural part of our human experience. All of us pray. Sometimes we pray only when we are at the peak of our powers and simply must thank someone; and sometimes we pray when we are at the very depth of despair and we simply cry out to God in our agony. Both of these times of prayer are natural and appropriate. But they are not enough to sustain us or to nurture our relationship with God.

Therefore we, as Wesley before us, Luther before him, Augustine before him, and Jesus before them all, need to establish a disciplined life of prayer. Since each of us is a unique creation of God, our life of prayer will be unique as well. We may each pray at different times, use different resources, pray for different lengths of time, pray more in solitude or pray more in community. It is important to recognize our differences as we fashion our way of living prayerfully.

Prayer is God's greatest provision for our spiritual life. Our relationship with God is impossible without prayer. We cannot know God's mind or heart without prayer. We cannot receive God's direction, hear God's voice, or respond to God's call without prayer. Since this is true, prayer is also God's greatest provision for all of life. It is the supreme means of grace given to all humankind.

Prayer was so very important for Jesus that he left even the needy crowd to pray (Mark 6:31). It was so important to Wesley that he established a rigorous discipline of prayer, lest this lifeline to God be broken and life itself be lost.

How important is this means of grace to you?

If, upon the closest search, you can find no sin of commission which causes the cloud upon your soul, inquire next, if there be not some sin of omission which separates between God and you.... Do you walk in all the ordinances of God? In public, family, private prayer? If not, if you habitually neglect any of these known duties, how can you expect that the light of his countenance should continue to shine upon you? ... When you hear a voice behind you saying, "This is the way, walk thou in it," harden not your heart: be no more "disobedient to the heavenly calling." Till the sin, whether of omission or commission, be removed, all comfort is false and deceitful. It is only skinning the wound over, which still festers and rankles beneath. Look for no peace within, till you are at peace with God; which cannot be without "fruits meet for repentance." *Sermon 46, The Wilderness State, Vol. 6, p. 86*

In a Christian believer *love* sits upon the throne which is erected in the inmost soul; namely, love of God and man, which fills the whole heart, and reigns without a rival. In a circle near the throne are all holy tempers: — longsuffering, gentleness, meekness, fidelity, temperance: and if any other were comprised in "the mind which was in Christ Jesus." In an exterior circle are all the *works of mercy*, whether to the souls or bodies of men.... Next to these are those that are usually termed works of piety: — reading and hearing the word, public, family, private prayer, receiving the Lord's Supper, fasting or abstinence. Lastly, that his followers may the more effectually provoke one another to love, holy tempers, and good works, our blessed Lord has united them together in one body, the Church. *Sermon 92, On Zeal, Vol. 7, p. 60*

"But what good works are those, the practice of which you affirm to be necessary to sanctification?" First, all works of piety; such as public prayer, family prayer, and praying in our closet; receiving the supper of the Lord; searching the Scriptures, by hearing, reading, meditating; and using such a measure of fasting or abstinence as our bodily health allows. *Sermon 43, The Scripture Way of Salvation, Vol. 6, p. 51*

If it be possible for any direction to be more clear, it is that which God hath given us by the Apostle, with regard to prayer of every kind, public or private, and the blessing annexed thereto: "If any of you lack wisdom, let him ask of God, that giveth to all men liberally." *Sermon 16, The Means of Grace, Vol. 5, p. 192*

May we not endeavour, Secondly, to *instruct* them? to take care that every person who is under our roof have all such knowledge as is necessary to salvation? . . . and you should take care that they have some time every day for reading meditation, and prayer; and you should inquire whether they do actually employ that time in the exercises for which it is allowed. Neither should any day pass without family prayer, seriously and solemnly performed. *Sermon 94, On Family Religion Vol. 7, p. 81*

I went over to Kingswood, and spake largely to the children, as also on *Saturday* and *Sunday*. I found there had been a fresh revival of the work of God among them some months ago: But it was soon at an end, which I impute chiefly to their total neglect of private prayer. Without this, all the other means which they enjoyed could profit them nothing. *Journal, Vol. 3, p. 479*

In the evening we came to Stafford. The mistress of the house joined with us in family prayer. The next morning, one of the servants appeared deeply affected, as did the ostler before we went. Soon after breakfast, stepping into the stable, I spake a few words with those who were there. A stranger who heard me said, "Sir I wish I was to travel with you:" and when I went into the house, followed me, and began abruptly, "Sir, I believe you are a good man, and I come to tell you a little of my life." The tears stood in his eyes all the time he spoke; and we hoped not a word which was said to him was lost. *Journal, Vol. 1, p. 87*

We came in the evening to Boroughbridge, where, to my great surprise, the mistress of the house, though much of a gentlewoman, desired she and her family might join with us in prayer. They did so likewise between four and five in the morning. Perhaps even this seed may bring forth fruit. *Journal, Vol. 1, p. 374*

Margaret Roper, about eight years old, has been thoughtful for some time. The other day, while they were at family-prayer, she burst into tears and wept bitterly. They asked, what was the matter. She said she was a great sinner, and durst not pray. They bade her go to bed. She no sooner came into the chamber than she began crying, and clapping her hands, so that they heard her across the street; but God soon bound up her broken heart. Being asked how she felt herself, she said, "Ten times better. Now I can love God. I wish you would sit up and sing with me all night." She has been happy ever since, and as serious as one of forty. *Journal, Vol. 3, p. 105*

May it not be one of the consequences of this, that so many of you are a generation of triflers: triflers with God, with one another, and with your own souls? For, how few of you spend, from one week to another, a single hour in private prayer! How few have any thought of God in the general tenor of your conversation! Who of you is, in any degree, acquainted with the work of his Spirit, his supernatural work in the souls of men? *Sermon 4, Scriptural Christianity, Vol. 5, p. 51*

For Wesley, the chief instituted means of grace was prayer. It is not exaggerating to say that he lived to pray and prayed to live. He called prayer "the grand means of drawing near to God." Prayer had this importance because Wesley understood the Christian faith as a life lived in relationship with God through Jesus Christ. Because this is so, prayer was the key to maintaining that relationship. Furthermore, the absence of prayer was seen by Wesley to be the most common cause of spiritual dryness. Nothing could substitute for prayer in maintaining the spiritual life.

Consequently, when we speak of the devotional life, we must begin with prayer. It is the "spiritual breathing" which sustains our life in Christ. It is the divine gift of communication and communion with our Creator. . . .

Wesley was no recluse. He did not live a monastic or detached life. On the contrary, he kept a schedule of work, writing, preaching, and traveling that is impressive even by today's standards. Obviously he did not withdraw each hour for devotional exercises. Instead, Wesley cultivated the habit *internally*. He learned to be fully engaged in the affairs of life and simultaneously involved in prayer to God. Wesley had trained himself to turn his "inner voice" to the Creator.

This is the true meaning of Paul's exhortation to pray without ceasing. . . .

Wesley expressed the full range of prayer. He praised, confessed, gave thanks, interceded for others, and let his own requests be made known unto God. Through such prayers, Wesley expressed the full range of emotions: joy, sorrow, compassion, concern, trust. One of the most striking features of his praying was honesty. Often Wesley bared his soul before God in doubts, questions, and even cries of anguish. When he was undergoing trials in Georgia, especially in his relation to Sophie Hopkey, Wesley recorded that he tried to pray, but could not. In that moment God seemed beyond reach, and he did not try to cover up the feeling with pious, artificial words. Consequently, Wesley's prayers have the ring of reality. When he prays with warmth and affection, we can know he is being genuine. When he records that his prayers were cold or indifferent, we can identify with him. In both dimensions we have a realistic guide. *Steve Harper, Devotional Life in the Wesleyan Tradition, pp. 19, 22, 25*

2

Scriptural Christianity

❖— *Scripture Sentence*
There is one body and one Spirit, just as you were
called to the one hope of your calling, one Lord, one
faith, one baptism, one God and Father of all, who is
above all and through all and in all. *Ephesians 4:4-7*

❖— *Scripture Readings*

Acts 2:37-42
Acts 2:43-47
Matthew 16:13-20
Matthew 5:1-16 ·

Acts 9:26-31
*Ephesians 3:1-20
Matthew 6:25-34

❖— *Silence for Meditation*

❖— *Spiritual Reading*

❖— *Recording Insights and Commitments*

❖— *Prayers of Thanks, Intercession, Petition, and Praise*

❖— *Hymn Portion*
The meek and lowly heart that in our Savior was, to
us that Spirit doth impart and signs us with his cross.
UMH #372

❖— *Offering All of Life to God*

❖— *Closing Affirmation*
Come to him, a living stone, though rejected by mor-
tals yet chosen and precious in God's sight, and like
living stones, let yourselves be built into a spiritual
house. *1 Peter 2:4-5*

─── *Reflections* ───

What is the "true north" for the Christian? Where do Christians get their bearing, their map for faithfulness? How should life be lived as a Christian? Where does one find direction in seeking to live the faithful life? All of these questions find their simple and profound answer in the phrase "scriptural Christianity." John Wesley relied on scripture as both compass, or source of direction, and sustenance, or source of spiritual food, for the earnest Christian. He believed that the "primitive church" drew its guidance from the Bible and the activity of the Holy Spirit within the community of believers. Primitive church or primitive Christianity meant, for Wesley, the church of the apostles and the first three centuries. For him, this was a kind of golden age, or model, for the church.

From the very earliest the Methodist movement was marked by this intense and focused desire to help all who desired it to live out the principles and practices of scriptural Christianity. This was not a political decision, but a spiritual and practical decision. This was not the action of a political discontent, but the decision of a heart yearning for and touched by God. As long as he lived, John Wesley continued to respect and borrow from the Anglican church of his time. But he was convinced that much of the primitive church had been lost or overlaid with human inventions. So, his intention, and that of the Holy Club and those who were to follow, was to go deeper and draw closer to God.

The desire of these early Methodists was to live in constant companionship and faithfulness with the living Christ. This was not an effort to separate themselves from the Anglican church or to injure the church or those within it. It was a simple desire to draw closer to God and to live in greater faithfulness to God. John Wesley believed that the key to this kind of life was to be found in the scriptures. Because he believed that his denomination reflected, more nearly than any other, the heart of scriptural Christianity, he continued to live in assent "to all doctrines ... observed all the rubric in the Liturgy ... even at the peril of my life" (*Farther Thoughts on Separation from the Church*). And yet he saw that without a sharpened focus on God and faithfulness to God, Christians would miss or, worse, lose their inheritance as children of God.

John Wesley was dismayed that those who professed to be Christians looked so much like those who made no profession of faith. He noted that the only observable difference was in opinions and modes of worship. But that is where the distinction ended. Radical and unqualified commitment to Christ was scarce, and therefore little observable fruit appeared in the life of the church. His emphasis on grace and holiness was an effort to change all of that. He believed that God would provide the necessary direction and power to live a distinctive life of holiness, if Christians utilized the means of grace that were available to all.

The fears that Wesley had for his time are shared by many in our time. It is not easy to find within any denomination in our time the essential core of scriptural Christianity that marked the primitive church. The "pure gold" of that primitive church has dimmed in our time as in Wesley's. We are often preoccupied with good but not essential things. It is not uncommon for the church in our time to have worthy goals, but no means to achieve them. Or, to have an honest desire to be faithful, but no carefully considered and taught way to access the means of grace that lead to faithfulness. And it is not uncommon for the church to be focused on itself and not on God as made known to us in Jesus Christ.

In other words, there is as great a need for scriptural Christianity in our time as there was in Wesley's time. We easily profess that the resources of grace are as available to us as they were to Wesley, but we find it difficult to find the fruits of that profession. Perhaps the primary question for us is about our desire to live a life of radical faithfulness. To determine to know nothing but Christ and the power of his salvation is to set out on a path that will lead to faithfulness. It will also lead to the same misunderstanding and ridicule that early Methodists experienced.

A life of personal and social holiness is as much a rarity in our time as in Wesley's. Now, as then, such a life will be misunderstood and will find opposition and mockery surrounding its practice. And yet, it is this determination to know God and be faithful to God that alone can lead to the fruit of scriptural Christianity. That fruit includes the comfort, assurance, fruitfulness, peace, and power promised to every faithful disciple. This is our inheritance as Christians. The way of scriptural Christianity also includes practicing the means of grace that lead one in the direction of personal and social holiness. An earnest commitment to walking with Christ always brings us to the road that leads to holiness, faithfulness, and God. Do we really want to be on any other road?

── *Spiritual Reading* ──

But how contrary is this scriptural account of the ancient Christians to the ordinary apprehensions of men! We have been apt to imagine, that the Primitive Church was all excellence and perfection; answerable to that strong description which St. Peter cites from Moses: "Ye are a chosen generation, a royal priesthood, a holy nation, a peculiar people." And such, without all doubt, the first Christian Church, which commenced at the day of Pentecost, was. But how soon did the fine gold become dim! How soon was the wine mixed with water! How little time elapsed, before the "god of this world" so far regained his empire, that Christians in general were scarce distinguishable from Heathens, save by their opinions and modes of worship! *Sermon 61, The Mystery of Iniquity, Vol. 6, p. 260*

What do you mean by order? a plan of church-discipline? What plan? the scriptural, the primitive, or our own? It is in the last sense of the word that I have been generally charged with breaking or setting aside order: that is, the rules of our own Church, both by preaching in the fields, and by using extemporary prayer. *Letter to John Smith, Vol. 12, p. 80*

From a child I was taught to love and reverence the Scripture, the oracles of God; and, next to these, to esteem the primitive Fathers, the writers of the first three centuries. Next after the primitive church, I esteemed our own, the Church of England, as the most scriptural national Church in the world. I therefore not only assented to all the doctrines, but observed all the rubric in the Liturgy, and that with all possible exactness, even at the peril of my life. *Farther Thoughts on Separation from the Church, Vol. 13, p. 272*

A few young gentlemen then at Oxford approved of and followed the advice. They were all zealous Churchmen, and both orthodox and regular to the highest degree. For their exact regularity they were soon nicknamed Methodists; but they were not then, or for some years after, charged with any other crime, real or pretended, than that of being right-

eous over much. Nine or ten years after, many others "united together in the several parts of the kingdom, engaging,
in like manner, to be helpful to each other in all good,
Christian ways." At first, all these were of the Church; but
several pious Dissenters soon desired to unite with them.
Their one design was, to forward each other in true, scriptural Christianity. *Letter to Mr. T.H., Vol. 13, p. 388*

It has, indeed, been proposed to desire the English Bishops
to ordain part of our Preachers for America. But to this I
object. . . . As our American brethren are now totally disen-
tangled both from the State, and from the English hierarchy,
we dare not entangle them again, either with the one or the
other. They are now at full liberty, simply to follow the
Scriptures and the primitive church. And we judge it best
that they should stand fast in that liberty wherewith God
has so strangely made them free. *Letter to Coke, Asbury, and
North American Brethren, Vol. 13, p. 252*

Judge not one another; but every man look into his own
bosom. How stands the matter in your own breast?
Examine your conscience before God. Are you an happy
partaker of this scriptural, this truly primitive, religion? Are
you a witness of the religion of love? Are you a lover of God
and all mankind? Does your heart glow with gratitude to
the Giver of every good and perfect gift. . . . Do you "walk
in love, as Christ also loved us, and gave himself for us?"
Do you, as you have time, "do good unto all men;" and in
as high a degree as you are able? . . . Whosoever thou art,
whose heart is herein as my heart, give me thine hand!
Come and let us magnify the Lord together, and labour to
promote his kingdom upon earth! Let us join hearts and
hands in this blessed work, in striving to bring glory to God
in the highest, by establishing peace and good will among
men, to the uttermost of our power! . . . Then let us endeavour to promote, in our several stations, this scriptural, primitive, religion; let us, with all diligence, diffuse the religion
of love among all we have any intercourse with; let us provoke all men, not to enmity and contention, but to love and
to good works; always remembering those deep words,
(God engrave them on all our hearts!) "God is love; and he
that dwelleth in love dwelleth in God, and God in him!"

Sermon 132, On Laying the Foundation of the New Chapel, Vol. 7, p. 430

But you will naturally ask, "What is Methodism? What does this new word mean? Is it not a new religion?" This is a very common, nay, almost an universal, supposition; but nothing can be more remote from the truth. It is a mistake all over. Methodism, so called, is the old religion, the religion of the Bible, the religion of the primitive Church, the religion of the Church of England. This old religion, (as I observed in the "Earnest Appeal to Men of Reason and Religion,") is "no other than love, the love of God and of all mankind; the loving God with all our heart, and soul, and strength, as having first loved us,—as the fountain of all the good we have received, and of all we ever hope to enjoy; and the loving every soul which God hath made, every man on earth as our own soul." *Sermon 132, On Laying the Foundation of the New Chapel, Vol. 7, p. 423*

Is it any wonder that we find so few Christians: for where is Christian discipline? In what part of England (to go no farther) is Christian discipline added to Christian doctrine? Now, whatever doctrine is preached, where there is not discipline, it cannot have its full effect upon the hearers. *Sermon 116, Causes of the Inefficacy of Christianity, Vol. 7, p. 285*

It would be easy to show, in how many respects the Methodists, in general, are deplorably wanting in the practice of Christian self-denial: from which, indeed, they have been continually frighted by the silly outcries of the Antinomians. To instance only in one: While we were at Oxford, the rule of every Methodist was, (unless in case of sickness) to fast every Wednesday and Friday of the year, in imitation of the Primitive Church: for which they had the highest reverence. Now this practice of the Primitive Church is universally allowed. "Who does not know," says Epiphanius, an ancient writer, "that the fasts of the fourth and sixth days of the week" (Wednesday and Friday) "are observed by the Christians throughout the world?" So they were by the Methodists for several years: by them all, without any exception; but afterwards, some in London carried this to excess, and fasted so as to impair their health. It was not long before others made this a pretence for not fasting at all. And I fear there are now thousands of Methodists, so called, both in England and Ireland, who, following the same bad example, have entirely left off fasting; ... the man that never fasts is no more on the way to heaven than the man that never prays. *Sermon 116, Causes of the Inefficacy of Christianity, Vol. 7, pp. 288–89*

It is well known, that, in the primitive Church, there were women particularly appointed for this work.[Visiting the sick—ed.] Indeed there was one or more such in every Christian congregation under heaven. They were then termed Deaconesses, that is, servants: servants of the Church, and of its great Master. Such was Phebe, (mentioned by St. Paul, Rom. xvi.1.) "a Deaconess of the Church of Cenchrea." It is true, most of these were women in years, and well experienced in the work of God. But were the young wholly excluded from that service? No: Neither need they be, provided they know in whom they have believed; and show that they are holy of heart, by being holy in all manner of conversation. Such a Deaconess, if she answered her picture, was Mr. Law's Miranda. Would any one object to her visiting and relieving the sick and poor, because she was a woman; nay, and a young one too? Do any of you that are young desire to tread in her steps? Have you a pleasing form, an agreeable address? So much the better, if you are wholly devoted to God. He will use these, if your eye be single, to make your words strike the deeper. And while you minister to others, how many blessings may redound into your own bosom! *Sermon 98, On Visiting the Sick, Vol. 7, p. 126*

From the beginning, God has dealt with the human family through covenants: with Adam and Eve, Noah, Abraham, Sarah, and Hagar, Moses; with Deborah, Ruth, and Jeremiah and other prophets. In each covenant, God offered the chosen people the blessings of providence and commanded of them obedience to the divine will and way, that through them all the world should be blessed (Genesis 18:18;22:18). In the new covenant in Christ, yet another community of hope was called out and gathered up, with the same promise and condition renewed that all who believe and obey shall be saved and made ministers of Christ's righteousness. Our spiritual forebears stressed this biblical theme of covenant-making and covenant-keeping as central in Christian experience.

The biblical story is marred by disregarded covenants and disrupted moral order, by sin and rebellion, with the resulting tragedies of alienation, oppression, and disorder. In the gospel of the new covenant, God in Christ has provided a new basis for reconciliation: justification by faith and birth into a new life in the Spirit. This gift, marked by growth toward wholeness of life, is revealed in Christ who came not to be served but to serve (Mark 10:45) and to give his life for the world. Christ freely took the nature of a servant, carrying this servanthood to its utmost limits (Philippians 2:7).

God's self-revelation in the life, death, and resurrection of Jesus Christ summons the church to ministry in the world through witness by word and deed in light of the church's mission. The visible church of Christ as a faithful community of persons affirms the worth of all humanity and the value of interrelationship in all of God's creation.

In the midst of a sinful world, through the grace of God, we are brought to repentance and faith in Jesus Christ. We become aware of the presence and life-giving power of God's Holy Spirit. We live in confident expectation of the ultimate fulfillment of God's purpose.

We are called together for worship and fellowship and for the upbuilding of the Christian community. We advocate and work for the unity of the Christian church. We call persons into discipleship.

As servants of Christ we are sent into the world to engage in the struggle for justice and reconciliation. We seek to reveal the love of God for men, women, and children of all ethnic, racial, cultural, and national backgrounds and to demonstrate the healing power of the gospel with those who suffer. *The Book of Discipline of The United Methodist Church 1996, pp. 107–8 (Par. 101–3)*

3

The Appropriate Use of Money

❖— *Scripture Sentence*
Awe came upon everyone, because many wonders and signs were being done by the apostles. All who believed were together. . . . they would sell their possessions and goods and distribute the proceeds to all, as any had need. *Acts 2:43-44*

❖— *Scripture Readings*

Acts 2:43-47	Matthew 19:16-26
*Matthew 6:19-21	2 Corinthians 8:1-7
Matthew 12:33-37	2 Corinthians 9:6-15
Matthew 13:44	

❖— *Silence for Meditation*

❖— *Spiritual Reading*

❖— *Recording Insights and Commitments*

❖— *Prayers of Thanks, Intercession, Petition, and Praise*

❖— *Hymn Portion*
No overplus, or need, no rich or poor were there, content with daily bread where each enjoy'd his share; with every common blessing bless'd they nothing had, yet all possess'd. *The Unpublished Poetry of Charles Wesley, Vol. II, p. 296*

❖— *Offering All of Life to God*

❖— *Closing Affirmation*
Happy is everyone who fears the Lord, who walks in his ways. *Psalm 128:1*

———— *Reflections* ————

The gap between rich and poor was a constant source of irritation and pain to John Wesley. He was convinced that the scriptures taught that there was enough for everyone and that it was the responsibility of those who have to share with those who have not.

His sermons about money and the danger of riches were clear and reminiscent of the words of Jesus on the same subject. The message he proclaimed was good news and bad news. He encouraged hard work, good stewardship, and wise living that would lead to receiving wealth.

On the other hand, he spoke strongly against the accumulation of wealth and taught and practiced giving as essential to any appropriate use of the gift of wealth. He feared that the people called Methodist might contribute to the widening rather than narrowing of the gap between rich and poor.

Therefore, he gave away most of what he gathered through his own labors and after having given away everything but bare necessities he was unashamed to beg on behalf of the poor. He practiced what he preached and was willing to live as an example of the appropriate use of money. As Lovett Weems points out, "John Wesley was always clear that money is an excellent gift of God. He was careful to insist that it is the love of money, not money itself, which is the root of all evil."

This "excellent gift" was to be used to alleviate the suffering of humankind and to proclaim the reign of God. Money is the gift that made Wesley's extensive travel, correspondence, and publication possible. But money was never used for personal comfort and it was never accumulated for personal benefit. Money made it possible to send missionaries, build houses of prayer and praise, and address the social problems of poverty and injustice with words and deeds.

What is the underlying principle for the appropriate use of money? The strong conviction that all that we are and possess is really on loan to us. We are stewards who have responsibility for the wise investment of life and all its assets. All gifts given, including the gift of life, come from the hand of a loving God, but they are not to be used carelessly or as we please. Wesley believed that our covenant with God brings us into partnership with God. Our life and possessions are not our own. We are in partnership with the Lord, and it is the Lord who determines how we invest the good gifts God gives.

Thus, Wesley believed that when we purchase something unnecessary or extravagant, we steal from the poor and take bread from the hands of the hungry. Money is to be used to declare in word and deed the good news of God's amazing grace extended to all. When a believer gives all of life to God, the use of money is no longer a decision made by the believer alone. Once this transaction of faith has taken place, the use of money is at the direction of God and faithfulness demands obedience to that direction.

Today we live in a world of a dangerous and increasing chasm between rich and poor. But it can be otherwise. To follow Wesley's example is to begin to transform the world through the appropriate use of the money placed in our hands by God. What simple and yet concrete steps can we take today to seek to bridge the gap between rich and poor? How should we invest the life and the resources God has given? Make this issue a matter of prayer this week and record any insights or urgings that you feel, and then when clarity comes, obey God's leading. You will not be disappointed. Faithfulness brings its own reward.

————— *Spiritual Reading* —————

John Wesley was always clear that money is an excellent gift of God. He was careful to insist that it is the love of money, not money itself, which is the root of all evil. Yet Wesley became deeply concerned as he saw Methodists, "with few exceptions," growing wealthier and at the same time decreasing in grace as they increased in wealth.

To those early Methodists Wesley implored: "The Lord of all will ... inquire, 'How didst thou employ the worldly goods which I lodged in thy hands...? In what manner didst thou employ that comprehensive talent, money?' [By] first supplying thy own reasonable wants, together with those of the family; then restoring the remainder to me, through the poor, whom I had appointed to receive it."

Wesley formulated this philosophy of giving in the following terms: "What way then ... can we take that our money may not sink us to the nethermost hell? There is one way, and there is no other under heaven. If those who 'gain all they can' and 'save all they can' will likewise 'give all they can' then, the more they gain the more they will grow in grace, and the more treasure they will lay up in heaven." *Lovett Weems, Pocket Guide to John Wesley's Message Today, p. 73*

'Gain all you can.' Here we may speak like the children of the world: we meet them on their own ground. And it is our bounden duty to do this: we ought to gain all we can gain, without buying gold too dear, without paying more for it than it is worth. But this it is certain we ought not to do; we ought not to gain money at the expense of life, nor (which is in effect the same thing) at the expense of our health.... We are, secondly, to gain all we can without hurting our mind, any more than our body. For neither may we hurt this: we must preserve, at all events, the spirit of a healthful mind.... We are, thirdly, to gain all we can without hurting our neighbor. But this we may not, cannot do, if we love our neighbour as ourselves. We cannot, if we love every one as ourselves, hurt any one in his substance. We cannot devour the increase of his lands, and perhaps the lands and houses themselves, by gaming, by overgrown bills. Neither may we gain by hurting our neighbor in his body. Therefore, we may not sell anything which tends to impair health. *Sermon 50, The Use of Money, Vol. 6, pp. 126–28*

Having gained all you can, by honest wisdom, and unwearied diligence, the second rule of Christian prudence is, 'Save all you can.' Do not throw the precious talent into the sea: leave that folly to heathen philosophers. Do not throw it away in idle expenses, which is just the same as throwing it into the sea. Expend no part of it merely to gratify the desire of the flesh, the desire of the eye, or the pride of life.

Do not waste any part of so precious a talent, merely in gratifying the desires of the flesh; in procuring the pleasures of sense, of whatever kind; particularly, in enlarging the pleasure of tasting. I do not mean, avoid gluttony and drunkenness only: an honest Heathen would condemn these. But there is a regular, reputable kind of sensuality, an elegant epicurism, which does not immediately disorder the stomach, nor (sensibly at least) impair the understanding; and yet (to mention no other effects of it now) it cannot be maintained without considerable expense. Cut off all this expense! Despise delicacy and variety, and be content with what plain nature requires. *Sermon 50, The Use of Money, Vol. 6, p. 131*

❖

But let not any man imagine that he has done anything, barely by going thus far, by 'gaining and saving all he can,' if he were to stop here. All this is nothing, if a man go not forward, if he does not point all this at a farther end. Nor, indeed, can a man properly be said to save anything, if he only lays it up. You may as well throw your money into the sea, as bury it in the earth. And you may as well bury it in the earth, as in your chest, or in the Bank of England. Not to use, is effectually to throw it away. If, therefore, you would indeed 'make yourselves friends of the mammon of unrighteousness,' add the third rule to the two preceding. Having, first, gained all you can, and, secondly, saved all you can, then 'give all you can.'

In order to see the ground and reason of this, consider, when the Possessor of heaven and earth brought you into being, and placed you in this world, He placed you here, not as a proprietor, but a steward: as such He entrusted you, for a season, with goods of various kinds; but the sole property of these still rests in Him, nor can ever be alienated from Him. As you yourself are not your own, but His, such is, likewise, all that you enjoy. Such is your soul and your body, not your own, but God's. And so is your substance in particular. And He has told you, in the most clear and express terms, how you are to employ it for Him, in such a manner, that it may be all an holy sacrifice, acceptable through Christ Jesus. And this light, easy service, He hath promised to reward with an eternal weight of glory. *Sermon 50, The Use of Money, Vol. 6, p. 133*

❖

History has shown that Wesley had every reason to be concerned with what was happening to Methodists as they became more prosperous and moved out of the lowest social classes. Social historians have now documented what Wesley was beginning to feel—that "rising prosperity of the Methodists (particularly those of the Wesleyan connection) cut them off from the close sympathy with working" people.

Some of the most haunting words that I have come across are by C. Eric Lincoln: "You will work for them but not with them. Your heart will bleed for them but not your head or your hands. You will be their advocate but not their friend. You will sponsor them and their causes, but their cause is not your cause anymore because you are middle class."

That is a gap which cannot be bridged by ideas or doctrines but only by a changed heart and soul and mind to go with whatever stewardship philosophy we have. The testimony of the Wesleyan Revival is that the gap was bridged in a significant way and that it can be bridged in any time by God's faithful people. *Lovett H. Weems, Pocket Guide to John Wesley's Message Today, p. 79*

4

Life in Christ

❖— *Scripture Sentence*
As you therefore have received Christ Jesus the Lord, continue to live your lives in him. *Colossians 2:6*

❖— *Scripture Readings*

John 11:17-27
Acts 17:22-28
John 12:20-26
Philippians 2:1-11

Colossians 3:1-11
*Colossians 3:12-17
John 10:1-10

❖— *Silence for Meditation*

❖— *Spiritual Reading*

❖— *Recording Insights and Commitments*

❖— *Prayers of Thanks, Intercession, Petition, and Praise*

❖— *Hymn Portion*
Jesus, confirm my heart's desire to work and speak and think like thee; still let me guard the holy fire, and still stir up thy gift in me. *UMH #501*

❖— *Offering All of Life to God*

❖— *Closing Affirmation*
Blessed be the God and Father of our Lord Jesus Christ! By his great mercy he has given us a new birth into a living hope through the resurrection of Jesus Christ from the dead, and into an inheritance that is imperishable . . . kept in heaven for you. *1 Peter 1:3-4*

——— *Reflections* ———

Jesus declared, "I am the bread of life. Whoever comes to me will never be hungry, and whoever believes in me will never be thirsty" (John 6:35). On another occasion he said, "I came that they may have life, and have it abundantly" (John 10:10). Why then is it so hard to see this life abundant and eternal reflected in the church and in the lives of individual Christians? John Wesley seemed to believe that the answer is quite simple. We have not really feasted on the bread of life and we have not yet given ourselves completely to God in Christ.

While life in Christ includes the simple spiritual disciplines of regular worship, Bible study, prayer, participation in the Lord's Supper and doing good, that is not all that life in Christ includes. The persons who found their relationship with God unfulfilling, their Christianity incomplete, and their lives without meaning were not yet really "in Christ." They were not yet Christian. They may have started on the good way but they had not gone far enough to reap the benefits of being in Christ. The readings for this week begin to give some of the depth and breadth of what it meant for early Methodists to follow Christ and live in Christ.

Wesley believed that every person's life could be "hid with Christ in God, being joined to the Lord in one spirit." Such union with Christ required significant response from the believer and carried with it significant consequences. Life in Christ begins with deep faith in and an unqualified commitment to God. Our faith in and our practice of the ordinary spiritual disciplines, while worthy, is not enough. Our modest attempts to live a moral life fall far short of life in Christ. There is first this deep faith that Jesus Christ does love me, that he lived, died, and rose again for me, and today offers to me life abundant and eternal. It is such a faith that permits us to offer our lives to God without qualification.

To live in Christ is to give all that we are, have, and hope to become to God's gracious direction. This is to enter into "fellowship" with God in a new and nurturing way—a way that leads to assurance of salvation and life abundant and eternal. It is a way that leads to the confidence and comfort that only companionship with Jesus Christ can bring. And it is a way that leads to definite and decisive response on the part of the believer.

In a world where institutions and individuals seem to be unworthy of trust, the believer finds in God one who is completely trustworthy. Thus it is possible to offer one's life, without reservation, and as totally as we are able, to this trustworthy God. Because God can be trusted, we can give ourselves to God without fear or anxiety that we will be deceived or disappointed. This kind of trust leads more and more to the living out of our faith. Life in Christ not only brings assurance and hope, it also begins to show some of the characteristics of Christ within the life of the believer. It is to have the image of God within each of us restored and made visible to ourselves and to others.

We have often seen children take on the qualities of their parents and students begin to reflect in their lives the life and ways of their teachers. To live in an intimate relationship with Christ is to begin to act like Christ, to think like Christ, and to be Christ-like in all of our living. Life in Christ brings great gifts that so many times are left unclaimed by those of us who start the Christian journey but are quick to turn away from the fullness of life that is offered. Our inheritance of assurance, comfort, peace, life abundant and eternal is often not incorporated into our daily life. Because it is not, we live anxious, fearful and incomplete lives, and we begin to wonder what difference our faith really makes. Life in Christ changes all of that as we live in the presence and power of Jesus Christ.

A further consequence of life in Christ is the pursuit of the way of Christ. We seek to be faithful and obedient as Jesus Christ was obedient. We observe more closely the life of Jesus and try to incorporate his ways into our own. As we do this, we learn to love God and realize that we cannot truly love God without loving our neighbor.

When we can say "for to me, living is Christ" (Phil. 1:21), we will have begun a life journey of challenge, excitement, serenity, peace, power, and reward. All are gifts of God waiting to be claimed by those who find life in Christ.

——— *Spiritual Reading* ———

How different is the case, how vast the pre-eminence, of them that "walk by faith"! God, having "opened the eyes of their understanding," pours divine light into their soul: whereby they are enabled to "see Him that is invisible," to see God and the things of God. What their "eye had not seen, nor their ear heard, neither had it entered into their heart to conceive." God from time to time reveals to them by the "unction of the Holy One, which teacheth them of all things." Having "entered into the holiest by the blood of Jesus," by that "new and living way," and being joined into "the general assembly and church of the first born, and unto God the Judge of all, and Jesus the Mediator of the New Covenant," — each of these can say, "I live not, but Christ liveth in me:" I now live that life which "is hid with Christ in God;" "and when Christ, who is my life, shall appear, then I shall likewise appear with him in glory."
Sermon 113, Walking by Sight, Walking by Faith, Vol. 7, p. 260

And it is as impossible to satisfy such a soul, a soul that is athirst for God, the living God, with what the world accounts religion, as with what they account happiness. The religion of the world implies three things: (1) The doing no harm, the abstaining from outward sin; at least from such as is scandalous, as robbery, theft, common swearing, drunkenness: (2) The doing good, the relieving the poor; the being charitable, as it is called: (3) The using of the means of grace; at least the going to church and to the Lord's Supper. He in whom these three marks are found is termed by the world a religious man. But will this satisfy him who hungers after God? No: It is not food for his soul. He wants a religion of a nobler kind, a religion higher and deeper than this. He can no more feed on this poor, shallow, formal thing, than he can "fill his belly with the east wind." True, he is careful to abstain from the very appearance of evil: he is zealous of good works: he attends all the ordinances of God: But all this is not what he longs for. This is only the outside of that religion, which he insatiably hungers after. The knowledge of God in Christ Jesus: "the life which is hid with Christ in God:" the being "joined unto the Lord in one spirit:" the having "fellowship with the Father and the Son:" the "walking in the light as God is in the light:" the being "purified even as He is pure:" — this is the religion, the righteousness, he thirsts after: Nor can he rest, till he thus rests in God. *Sermon 22, Sermon on the Mount, Discourse 2, Vol. 5, p. 268*

He, therefore, who liveth in true believers, hath "purified their hearts by faith:" insomuch that every one that hath Christ in him the hope of glory, "purifieth himself, even as He is pure." (1 John iii.3) He is purified from pride; for Christ was lowly of heart. He is pure from self will or desire; for Christ desired only to do the will of his Father, and to finish his work. And he is pure from anger, in the common sense of the word; for Christ was meek and gentle, patient and longsuffering. *Sermon 40, Christian Perfection, Vol. 6, p. 17*

While a man is in a mere natural state, before he is born of God, he has, in a spiritual sense, eyes and sees not; a thick impenetrable veil lies upon them; he has ears, but hears not; he is utterly deaf to what he is most of all concerned to hear. His other spiritual senses are all locked up: He is in the same condition as if he had them not. Hence he has no knowledge of God; no intercourse with him; he is not at all acquainted with him. He has no true knowledge of the things of God, either of spiritual or eternal things; therefore, though he is a living man, he is a dead Christian. But as soon as he is born of God, there is a total change in all these particulars. The "eyes of his understanding are opened;" (such is the language of the great Apostle:) and, He who of old "commanded light to shine out of darkness shining on his heart, he sees the light of the glory of God," his glorious love, "in the face of Jesus Christ." His ears being opened, he is now capable of hearing the inward voice of God, saying, "Be of good cheer; thy sins are forgiven thee:" "go and sin no more." This is the purport of what God speaks to his heart; although perhaps not in these very words. He is now ready to hear whatsoever "He that teacheth man knowledge" is pleased, from time to time, to reveal to him. He "feels in his heart," to use the language of our Church, "the mighty working of the Spirit of God;" not in a gross, carnal, sense, as the men of the world stupidly and wilfully misunderstand the expression; though they have been told again and again, we mean thereby neither more nor less than this: He feels, is inwardly sensible of, the graces which the Spirit of God works in his heart. He feels, he is conscious of, a "peace which passeth all understanding." He many times feels such a joy in God as is "unspeakable, and full of glory." He feels "the love of God shed abroad in his heart by the Holy Ghost which is given unto him:" and all his spiritual senses are then exercised to discern spiritual good and evil. By the use of these, he is daily increasing in the knowledge of God, of Jesus Christ whom he hath sent, and of all the things pertaining to his inward kingdom. And now he may be properly said to live: God having quickened him by his Spirit, he is alive to God through Jesus Christ. *Sermon 45, The New Birth, Vol. 6, p. 70*

I have a higher demand upon you who love as well as fear God. He whom you fear, whom you love, has qualified you for promoting his work in a more excellent way. Because you love God, you love your brother also: You love, not only your friends, but your enemies: not only the friends, but even the enemies, of God. You have "put on, as the elect of God, lowliness, gentleness, longsuffering." You have faith in God, and in Jesus Christ whom he hath sent: faith which overcometh the world: And hereby you conquer both evil and shame, and that "fear of man which bringeth a snare:" so that you can stand with boldness before them that despise you, and make no account of your labors. Qualified, then, as you are, and armed for the fight, will you be like the children of Ephraim, "who, being harnessed, and carrying bows, turned back in the day of battle?" Will you leave a few of your brethren to stand alone, against all the hosts of the aliens? O say not, "This is too heavy a cross: I have not courage or strength to bear it." True; not of yourself: But you that believe "can do all things through Christ strengthening you." "If thou canst believe, all things are possible to him that believeth." No cross is too heavy for him to bear: knowing that they that "suffer with him shall reign with him." *Sermon 52, The Reformation of Manners, Vol. 6, p. 165*

From the preceding considerations we may learn the full answer to one of the grand objections of infidels against

Christianity: namely, *the lives of Christians*. Of Christians, do you say? I doubt whether you ever knew a *Christian* in your life. When Tomo Chachi, the Indian Chief, keenly replied to those who spoke to him of being a Christian, "Why, these are Christians at Savannah! These are Christians at Frederica!"—the proper answer was, "No, they are not; they are no more Christians than you and Sinauky." "But are not these Christians in Canterbury, in London, in Westminster?" No: no more than they are angels. None are Christians, but they that have the mind which was in Christ, and walk as he walked. "Why, if these only are Christians," said an eminent wit, "I never saw a Christian yet." I believe it: You never did: and, perhaps, you never will: for you will never find them in the grand ... world. The few Christians that are upon the earth, are only to be found where you never look for them. Never, therefore, urge this objection more: Never object to Christianity the lives or tempers of Heathens. Though they are called Christians, the name does not imply the thing: They are as far from this as hell from heaven. *Sermon 61, The Mystery of Iniquity, Vol. 6, p. 264*

He wilfully and openly rebelled against God, and cast off his allegiance to the Majesty of heaven. Hereby he instantly lost both the favour of God, and the image of God wherein he was created. As he was then incapable of obtaining happiness by the old, God established a new covenant with man; the terms of which were no longer, "Do this and live," but, "Believe, and thou shalt be saved." But still the end of man is one and the same; only it stands on another foundation. For the plain tenor of it is, "Believe in the Lord Jesus Christ, whom God hath given to be the propitiation for thy sins, and thou shalt be saved;" first, from the guilt of sin, having redemption through his blood; then from the power, which shall have no more dominion over thee; and then from the root of it, into the whole image of God. And being restored both to the favour and image of God, thou shalt know, love, and serve him to all eternity. So that still the end of his life, the life of every man born into the world, is to know, love, and serve his great Creator. *Sermon 109, What Is Man?, Vol. 7, p. 230*

5

Our Sovereign God

❖— *Scripture Sentence*
In the beginning when God created the heavens and the earth, the earth was a formless void and darkness covered the face of the deep, while a wind from God swept over the face of the waters.... God saw everything that he had made, and indeed, it was very good. *Genesis 1: 1-2, 31*

❖— *Scripture Readings*

John 1:1-18	Psalm 8
Genesis 17:1-8	Psalm 46
*Ephesians 1:3-14	2 Peter 1:3-11
Colossians 1:15-20	

❖— *Silence for Meditation*

❖— *Spiritual Reading*

❖— *Recording Insights and Commitments*

❖— *Prayers of Thanks, Intercession, Petition, and Praise*

❖— *Hymn Portion*
Maker, in whom we live, in whom we are and move, the glory, power, and praise receive for thy creating love. Let all the angel throng give thanks to God on high, while earth repeats the joyful song and echoes to the sky. *UMH #88*

❖— *Offering All of Life to God*

❖— *Closing Affirmation*
Where can I go from your spirit? Or where can I flee from your presence? If I ascend to heaven, you are there; If I make my bed in Sheol, you are there. If I take the wings of the morning and settle at the farthest limits of the sea, even there your hand shall lead me, and your right hand shall hold me fast. *Psalm 139: 7-10*

———— *Reflections* ————

The writer of the Psalms, observing the star-filled sky, was inspired to proclaim God's sovereignty in eloquent and persuasive ways in Psalm 46. Psalm 97 declares that the Lord is king and that God has the capacity to be God. Psalm 8 affirms God's power to create and care for all that has been created. The Psalms reflect the message of the entire Bible. God is sovereign and God is able.

In a world of almost instant communication and graphic story-telling about the tragedy and pain of the world, it is easy to forget this ancient truth. God is sovereign and therefore God is able to care for and provide for all of creation.

Once we lose the concept of God as sovereign, our prayers, our faith, and our very souls begin to shrink. To believe in a severely limited God takes the heart out of reverence and out of prayer. To stand before the Master of the Universe is quite different than to stand before a limited and often defeated god. To pray to one who has little interest and even less capacity to hear and answer prayer will result in a different kind of prayer life than to pray to the One who speaks all creation into being and cares intensely about even the smallest detail of creation, such as every hair upon our heads.

Commitment to a god that is too small will stifle any hope for a transformed world and dull our efforts to bring such a world into being. We become prisoners to our own weaknesses and the evil of the world when we forget that God is sovereign and God is able. Not only our salvation, but our prayers, our hope, our trust, our work, and our very lives are at risk when we follow a god too small to meet the needs of all of creation. Wesleyan theology never suffered from this weakness.

From the very beginning Wesley was clear about the sovereignty of God. He never doubted God's ability to care for and provide for all that God had created. God was omnipotent and there could never be any threat to God's power. Wesley did not minimize human responsibility but was always clear that God was sovereign and absolutely no worthy human endeavor could occur without God's participation. If God were to withhold participation, the creation itself would collapse.

Humankind is eternally linked to and empowered by God. In the spiritual reading for this week, Randy Maddox points out that God's grace works powerfully but not irresistibly. God does not rob us of our liberty and freedom or force us to walk in holiness. But God's grace does invite us compellingly and seek to persuade us powerfully to walk in companionship with the One who has made us and redeemed us.

If God is sovereign, then we can pray confidently and boldly for the redemption of the world, the conversion of evil to good, the transformation of a timid church to a faithful church, the renewal of a morally bankrupt society to one of justice and mercy, and the salvation of our own troubled souls. The God of nature, history, and the scriptures is sovereign and able to meet any need at any time.

Consequently, we are bold enough to pray for God's intervention in today's most difficult problems with the assurance that God is able to transform the weak and timid and to root out even the most deeply entrenched evil. Further, we can invest our energies and direct our lives on the pathway to social and personal holiness because we know that God is with us and is able to help us while defending us and always holding us close.

Prayers that are completely dependent upon a sovereign God will touch the most troubling parts of our lives and society as a whole. Once we begin to incorporate belief in a sovereign God into our lives, we will be unafraid to throw our energies into the struggle that seems overwhelming without God. What are you planning that will be certain to fail without God's intervention? What are you praying for that requires God's powerful and active participation to bring answer to your prayers? Questions such as these can reveal the smallness of our faith and our god. Wesleyan theology encourages us to trust and obey an omnipotent God who is Lord over all. Fear, anxiety, and hopelessness are driven from our lives, for this sovereign God loves us and is able to care for us. We can live confidently and faithfully because God is able to care for and provide for all of creation.

—— *Spiritual Reading* ——

And as the true God, he is also the Supporter of all the things that he hath made. He beareth, upholdeth, sustaineth, all created things by the word of his power, by the same powerful word which brought them out of nothing. As this was absolutely necessary for the beginning of their existence, it is equally so for the continuance of it: Were his almighty influence withdrawn, they could not subsist a moment longer. Hold up a stone in the air; the moment you withdraw your hand, it naturally falls to the ground. In like manner, were he to withdraw his hand for a moment, the creation would fall into nothing. *Sermon 77, Spiritual Worship, Vol. 6, p. 426*

But does not the Scripture teach, "The help which is done upon earth, God doeth it himself?" Most certainly he does. And he is able to do it by his own immediate power. He has no need of using any instruments at all, either in heaven or earth. He wants not either angels or men, to fulfil the whole counsel of his will. But it is not his pleasure so to work. He never did; and we may reasonably suppose he never will. He has always wrought by such instruments as he pleases: But still it is God himself that doeth the work. Whatever help, therefore, we have, either by angels or men, is as much the work of God, as if he were to put forth his almighty arm, and work without any means at all. But he has used them from the beginning of the world: In all ages he has used the ministry both of men and angels. And hereby, especially, is seen "the manifold wisdom of God in the Church." Meanwhile, the same glory redounds to him, as if he used no instruments at all. *Sermon 71, Of Good Angels, Vol. 6, p. 369*

Almighty and everlasting God, the sovereign Lord of all creatures in heaven and earth, we acknowledge that our beings, and all the comforts of them, depend on thee, the Fountain of all good. We have nothing but what is owing entirely to thy free and bounteous love, O most blessed Creator, and to the riches of thy grace, O most blessed Redeemer. *A Collection of Prayers for Families, Vol. 11, p. 245*

In a word, there is no point in space, whether within or without the bounds of creation, where God is not. Indeed, this subject is far too vast to be comprehended by the narrow limits of human understanding. We can only say, The great God, the eternal, the almighty Spirit, is as unbounded in his presence, as in his duration and power. *S e r m o n 111, On the Omnipresence of God, Vol. 7, p. 239*

It is a divine evidence and conviction, Secondly, that what God hath promised he is able to perform. Admitting, therefore, that "with men it is impossible to bring a clean thing out of an unclean," to purify the heart from all sin, and to fill it with all holiness; yet this creates no difficulty in the case, seeing "with God all things are possible." And surely no one ever imagined it was possible to any power less than that of the Almighty! But if God speaks, it shall be done.God saith, "Let there be light; and there" is "light!" *Sermon 43, The Scripture Way of Salvation, Vol. 6, p. 52*

We allow, likewise, that all outward means whatever, if separate from the Spirit of God, cannot profit at all, cannot conduce, in any degree, either to the knowledge or love of God. Without controversy, the help that is done upon earth, He doeth it himself. It is He alone who, by his own almighty power, worketh in us what is pleasing in his sight; and all outward things, unless He work in them and by them, are mere weak and beggarly elements. Whosoever, therefore, imagines there is any intrinsic power in any means whatsoever, does greatly err, not knowing the Scriptures, neither the power of God. We know that there is no inherent power in the words that are spoken in prayer, in the letter of Scripture read, the sound thereof heard, or the bread and wine received in the Lord's supper; but that it is God alone who is the Giver of every good gift, the Author of all grace; that the whole power is of Him, whereby, through any of these, there is any blessing conveyed to our souls. We know, likewise, that he is able to give the same grace, though there were no means on the face of the earth. In this sense, we may affirm that, with regard to God, there is no such thing as means.... *Sermon 16, The Means of Grace, Vol. 5, p. 188*

It has been frequently supposed, that there is another cause, if not of darkness, at least, of heaviness; namely, God's withdrawing himself from the soul, because it is his sovereign will. Certainly he will do this, if we grieve his Holy Spirit, either by outward or inward sin; either by doing evil, or neglecting to do good; by giving way either to pride or anger, to spiritual sloth, to foolish desire, or inordinate affection. But that he ever withdraws himself *because he will,* merely because it is his good pleasure, I absolutely deny. There is no text in all the Bible which gives any colour for such a supposition. Nay, it is a supposition contrary, not only to many particular texts, but to the whole tenor of Scripture. It is repugnant to the very nature of God: It is utterly beneath his majesty and wisdom, (as an eminent writer strongly expresses it,) "to play at bo-peep with his creatures." It is inconsistent both with his justice and mercy, and with the sound experience of all his children. *Sermon 47, Heaviness Through Manifold Temptation, Vol. 6, p. 98*

For he created man in his own image: A spirit like himself; a spirit endued with understanding, with will or affections, and liberty; without which, neither his understanding nor his affections could have been of any use, neither would he have been capable either of vice or virtue. He could not be a moral agent, any more than a tree or stone. If, therefore, God were thus to exert his power, there would certainly be no more vice; but it is equally certain, neither could there be any virtue in the world. Were human liberty taken away, men would be as incapable of virtue as stones. Therefore, (with reverence be it spoken) the Almighty himself cannot do this thing. He cannot thus contradict himself, or undo what he has done. He cannot destroy out of the soul of man that image of himself wherein he made him: And without doing this, he cannot abolish sin and pain out of the world. But were it to be done, it would imply no wisdom at all; but barely a stroke of omnipotence. Whereas all the manifold wisdom of God (as well as all his power and goodness) is displayed in governing man as man; not as a stock or stone, but as an intelligent and free spirit, capable of choosing either good or evil. Herein appears the depth of the wisdom of God, in his adorable providence; in governing men, so as not to destroy either their understanding, will, or liberty. He commands all things, both in heaven and earth, to assist man in attaining the end of his being, in working out his own salvation, so far as it can be done without compulsion, without over-ruling his liberty. An attentive inquirer may easily discern, the whole frame of divine providence is so constituted as to afford man every possible help, in order to his doing good and eschewing evil, which can be done without turning man into a machine; without making him incapable of virtue or vice, reward or punishment. *Sermon 67, On Divine Providence, Vol. 6, p. 318*

No issue concerning God's nature received more attention from Wesley than that of Divine sovereignty. Central to his various discussions of this issue was the insistence that Divine sovereignty not be understood in isolation from God's other attributes. In particular, it must never be understood in abstraction from God's justice or love. Involved here is a perennial debate concerning whether God's will defines what is right, or the right determines what God wills. While Wesley professed little patience with this debate, his consideration of it rejected the nominalists' suggestion that God's will can be considered apart from God's nature.

Such emphasis on the unity of God's nature and will (i.e., God's simplicity) has far-reaching implications for understanding God's omnipotence. Wesley could define this attribute in fairly traditional terms, as the exclusion of any bounds to God's power. Whenever he developed this point however, it became clear that his distinctive concern was that God's power not be defined or defended in any way that undercuts human responsibility.

Wesley discerned such a mistaken conception of Divine power in the claims of his predestinarian opponents that they preserved the glory of God better than he did. Their obvious assumption was that one could ascribe the full glory of salvation to God only if God alone effected salvation, without human concurrence. Wesley countered that affirming a place for (uncoerced) human response in salvation did not detract from God's glory, provided it was God's grace which enabled humans to respond. Moreover, he charged, the biblical notion of the "glory of God" does not refer primarily to God's power, it refers to the manifestation of all God's attributes, and especially justice and love!...

What then is the proper understanding of God's power or sovereignty? Wesley utilized a distinction between God's work as Creator and as Governor to answer this question. He allowed that it may be permissible to speak of God working alone and irresistibly when creating and sustaining nonpersonal nature, but not when governing human life—for this would eliminate human responsibility. As Governor, God enables human obedience, but will not force it. As Wesley reminded his followers,

> You know how God wrought in *your own* soul when he first enabled you to say, "The life I now live, I live by faith in the Son of God, who loved me, and gave himself for me." He did not take away your understanding, but enlightened and strengthened it. He did not destroy any of your affections; rather they were more vigorous than before. Least of all did he take away your liberty, your power of choosing good or evil; he did not force you; but being *assisted* by his grace you ... *chose* the better part.

Perhaps the best way to capture Wesley's conviction here is to say that he construed God's power of sovereignty fundamentally in terms of *empowerment*, rather than control or overpowerment. This is not to weaken God's power, but to determine its character! As Wesley was fond of saying, God works "strongly and sweetly." That is, God's grace works powerfully, but not irresistibly, in matters of human life and salvation; thereby empowering our response-ability, without overriding our responsibility. While such an understanding of God's power may be less typical in the West, it is quite similar to central Eastern Orthodox emphases. *Randy L. Maddox, Responsible Grace: John Wesley's Practical Theology, pp. 54–55*

6

Good Stewards of Time

❖— *Scripture Sentence*
Keep alert, stand firm in your faith, be courageous, be strong. Let all that you do be done in love. *1 Corinthians 16:13-14*

❖— *Scripture Readings*

Matthew 26:36-46	Psalm 119:121-128
Haggai 1:1-11	Colossians 4:1-6
*Romans 13:11-14	Ephesians 5:1-20
John 7:1-13	

❖— *Silence for Meditation*

❖— *Spiritual Reading*

❖— *Recording Insights and Commitments*

❖— *Prayers of Thanks, Intercession, Petition, and Praise*

❖— *Hymn Portion*
I'll praise my Maker while I've breath; and when my voice is lost in death, praise shall employ my nobler powers. My days of praise shall ne'er be past, while life, and thought, and being last, or immortality endures. *UMH #60*

❖— *Offering All of Life to God*

❖— *Closing Affirmation*
While we have time, let us do good to all. *John Wesley, Letter, Vol. 1, p. 9*

———— *Reflections* ————

The wisdom to use the gift of time well is one of the reasons John Wesley was so influential in his own era and still remains a significant contributor to Christian thought today. He had the ability to do the work at hand and avoid the paralysis of being "swamped" by the work that remained. With all of his energy, creativity and, some would say, compulsion to get things done, he was still able to live the moment fully. To make the most of the present moment and to trust God for the rest was a quality that marked his entire ministry.

While there is evidence of (and regret for) occasional procrastination and not seizing the moment, for the most part, Wesley avoided "adjourning to a time that never came." He was critical of himself and others who were content to wait for a more appropriate time to come to saving faith or to live out that faith in daily life. The present moment was the only one anyone had and the moment in which to respond to God's call and commission.

The biblical witness is that each of our days is numbered. We know that some will complete their sojourn here in this world soon and others late. All of our days are in God's hands. However, for the days given, each of us has the same number of hours in every day. Time is one of the few gifts that is given equally to each of us every day. No one receives more than another and no one receives a higher quality of time than any other. We receive this gift as individuals with unique qualities and characteristics, and we each receive the gift in a unique and different context. But the gift of time itself is given to each in equal measure.

How then are we to use this gift appropriately? From observing the Wesley family and reading what John and Charles wrote, we learn some of the principles that seemed to guide them. First of all was the constant endeavor to use every moment wisely. That meant to be about life's most important work, which was knowing God and obeying God's direction. Everything else was secondary. To walk faithfully with God in Christ and to give oneself fully to the mission of Christ in the world was always the priority.

Therefore every day was marked with prayer, reading and reflecting upon scripture, witness to the saving power and presence of God in the world. Every day was also marked by acts of mercy and compassion to God's children regardless of their circumstance, but especially to the poor and neglected. If time remained, it was to be used for study, rest, and preparing oneself for more faithful discipleship. While we may know more about the importance of rest, Sabbath, and leisure for each of us than the Wesleys did, we have much to learn from them about the way we spend the precious gift of time.

———— *Spiritual Reading* ————

There is no employment of our time, no action or conversation, that is purely indifferent. All is good or bad, because all our time, as every thing we have, is not our own. All these are, as our Lord speaks, *ta allotria,—the property of another:* of God our Creator. Now, these either are or are not employed according to his will. If they are so employed, all is good: if they are not, all is evil. Again: It is his will, that we should continually grow in grace, and in the living knowledge of our Lord Jesus Christ. Consequently, every thought, word, and work, whereby this knowledge is increased, whereby we grow in grace, is good; and every one whereby this knowledge is not increased, is truly and properly evil. *Sermon 51, The Good Steward, Vol. 6, p. 148*

My scraps of time this week I employed in setting down my present thoughts upon a single life, which, indeed, are just the same they have been these thirty years; and the same they must be, unless I give up my Bible. *Journal, Vol. 3, p. 201*

All my leisure time during my stay at Bristol, I employed in finishing the fourth volume of "Discourses:" probably the last which I shall publish.... I walked up to Knowle, a mile from Bristol, to see the French prisoners. Above eleven hundred of them, we were informed, were confined in that little place without any thing to lie on but a little dirty straw, or any thing to cover them but a few foul thin rags, either by day or night, so that they died like rotten sheep. I was much affected, and preached in the evening on, (Exodus xxiii.9) "Thou shalt not oppress a stranger; for ye know the heart of a stranger, seeing ye were strangers in the land of Egypt." Eighteen pounds were contributed immediately, which were made up four-and-twenty the next day. With this we bought linen and woolen cloth, which were made up into shirts, waistcoats, and breeches. Some dozen of stockings were added; all which were carefully distributed, where there was greatest want. Presently after, the Corporation of Bristol sent a large quantity of mattresses and blankets. *Journal, Vol. 2, p. 516*

While these indefatigable Ministers of Christ were thus exerting themselves to promote a general revival of pure religion, the Preachers under their direction, though labouring in more limited districts of country, were scarcely less laboriously employed. At this period one of them writes from Lancashire to Mr. Wesley:—"Many doors are opened for preaching in these parts, but cannot be supplied for want of Preachers. I think some one should be sent to assist me, otherwise we shall lose ground. My Circuit requires me to travel one hundred and fifty miles in two weeks; during which time I preach publicly thirty-four times, besides meeting the societies, visiting the sick, and transacting other affairs." *The Life of the Rev. John Wesley, Vol. 5, p. 524*

I preached at Bury; and on Wednesday, at Colchester, where I spent a day or two with much satisfaction, among a poor, loving, simple-hearted people. I returned to London on Friday, and was fully employed in visiting the classes from that time to Saturday. *Journal, Vol. 4, p. 4*

At ten (and so every morning) I met the Preachers that were in town, and read over with them the "Survey of the Wisdom of God in the Creation." Many pupils I had at the University, and I took some pains with them: But to what effect? What is to become of them now? How many of them think either of their Tutor or their God? But, blessed be God! I have had some pupils since, who well reward me for my labour. Now "I live;" for "ye stand fast in the Lord." *Journal, Vol. 3, p. 201*

But not to avail ourselves of authority, let us weigh the thing in the balance of reason. I ask, What can make a wicked man happy? You answer, "He has gained the whole world." We allow it; and what does this imply? He has gained all that gratifies the senses: In particular, all that can please the taste; all the delicacies of meat and drink. True; but can eating and drinking make a man happy? They never did yet: And certain it is, they never will. This is too coarse a food for an immortal spirit. But suppose it did give him a poor kind of happiness, during those moments wherein he was swallowing; what will he do with the residue of his time? Will it not hang heavy upon his hands? Will he not groan under many a tedious hour, and think swift-winged time flies too slow? If he is not fully employed, will he not frequently complain of lowness of spirits? an unmeaning expression; which the miserable physician usually no more understands than his miserable patient. *Sermon 84, The Important Question, Vol. 6, p. 501*

Yet it is certain there is business to be done: And many we find in all places (not to speak of the vulgar, the drudges of the earth) who are continually employed therein. Are you of that number? Are you engaged in trade, or some other reputable employment? I suppose, profitable, too; for you would not spend your time and labour and thought for nothing. You are then making your fortune; you are getting money. True; but money is not your ultimate end. The treasuring up gold and silver, for its own sake, all men own, is as foolish and absurd, as grossly unreasonable, as the treasuring up spiders, or the wings of butterflies. You consider this but as a means to some farther end. And what is that? Why, the enjoying yourself, the being at ease, the taking your pleasure, the living like a gentleman; that is, plainly, either the whole or some part of the happiness above described. *An Earnest Appeal to Men of Reason and Religion, Vol. 8, p. 17*

I answer, (1.) Gaining knowledge is a good thing; but saving souls is a better. (2.) By this very thing you will gain the most excellent knowledge, that of God and eternity. (3.) You will have time for gaining other knowledge, too, if you spend all your mornings therein. Only sleep not more than you need; and never be idle, or triflingly employed. But, (4.) If you can do but one, let your studies alone. I would throw by all the libraries in the world, rather than be guilty of the loss of one soul. *Minutes of Several Conversations, Vol. 8, p. 304*

In November, 1729, at which time I came to reside at Oxford, your son, my brother, myself, and one more, agreed to spend three or four evenings in a week together. Our design was to read over the classics, which we had before read in private, on common nights, and on Sunday some book in divinity. In the summer following, Mr. M. told me he had called at the gaol, to see a man who was condemned for killing his wife; and that, from the talk he had with one of the debtors, he verily believed it would do much good, if any one would be at the pains of now and then speaking with them. This he so frequently repeated, that on the 24th of August, 1730, my brother and I walked with him to the castle. We were so well satisfied with our conversation there, that we agreed to go thither once or twice a week; which we had not done long, before he desired me to go with him to see a poor woman in the town, who was sick. In this employment, too, when we came to reflect upon it, we believed it would be worth while to spend an hour or two in a week. *Introductory Letter, Vol. 1, p. 6*

I do not remember that we met with any person who answered any of these questions in the negative; or who even doubted, whether it were not lawful to apply to this use that time and money which we should else have spent in other diversions. But several we met with who increased our little stock of money for the prisoners and the poor, by subscribing something quarterly to it; so that the more persons we proposed our designs to, the more we were confirmed in the belief of their innocency, and the more determined to pursue them, in spite of the ridicule, which increased fast upon us during the winter. *Introductory Letter, Vol. 1, p. 12*

(We) "have not so learned Christ," as to renounce any part of his service, though men should "say all manner of evil against us," with more judgment and as little truth as hitherto. We do indeed, use all the lawful means we know, to prevent the "good which is in us from being evil spoken of:" But if the neglect of known duties be the one condition of securing our reputation, why, fare it well; we know whom we have believed, and what we thus lay out He will pay us again. Your son already stands before the judgment-seat of Him who judges righteous judgment; at the brightness of whose presence the clouds remove: His eyes are open, and he sees clearly whether it was "blind zeal, and a thorough mistake of true religion, that hurried him on in the error of his way;" or whether he acted like a faithful and wise servant, who, from a just sense that his time was short, made haste to finish his work before his Lord's coming, that "when laid in the balance" he might not "be found wanting." *Introductory Letter, Vol. 1, p.14*

I had leisure to reflect on the strange case of Francis Coxon, who was at first the grand support of the society at Biddick. But after a time he grew weary of well-doing; complaining that it took up too much of his time. He then began to search after curious knowledge, and to converse with those who were like-minded. The world observed it, and courted his company again. Now he was not so precise; his school was filled with children; money flowed in, and he said, "Soul, take thy ease for many years." He came to Newcastle with John Reah the Saturday after I came; but had no leisure to call upon me. At night they set out homeward. He was walking a little before his companion, about three miles from Newcastle, in a way he knew as well as his own house-floor, when John heard him fall, and asked, "What is the matter?" He answered, "God has overtaken me: I am fallen into the quarry, and have broke my leg." John ran to some houses that were near, and, having procured help, carried him thither. Thence he was removed to another house, and a Surgeon sent for, who came immediately. He soon recovered his spirits, and asked how long it would be, before he could be in his school again. And on Sunday, Monday, and Tuesday, was full of the world, nor was God in all his thoughts. On Wednesday, the Surgeon told him honestly, he thought he could not live. Then he awoke out of sleep. *Journal, Vol. 2, p. 50*

Finding my fever greatly increased, I judged it would be best to keep my bed, and to live awhile on apples and apple-tea. On *Tuesday*, I was quite well, and should have preached, but that Dr. Rutty (who had been with me twice) insisted on my resting for a time. *Journal, Vol. 2, p. 94*

I spent a little time in a visit to Mr. M—; twenty years ago a zealous and useful Magistrate, now a picture of human nature in disgrace; feeble in body and mind; slow of speech and understanding. Lord, let me not live to be useless! *Journal, Vol. 3, p. 158*

It was in pursuance of an advice given by Bishop Taylor, in his "Rules for Holy Living and Dying," that, about fifteen years ago, I began to take a more exact account than I had done before, of the manner wherein I spent my time, writing down how I had employed every hour. This I continued to do wherever I was, till the time of my leaving England. The variety of scenes which I then passed through, induced me to transcribe, from time to time, the more material parts of my diary, adding here and there such little reflections as occurred to my mind. *Preface, Vol. 1, p. 2*

Mr. H., one of the first ten who met in band with my brother and me, desired to speak with me. I had not exchanged a word with him before, since we parted at Fetter-Lane. He said, about six years ago, the Brethren told him, it was the will of the Lamb, that he should give himself to the public work, quitting all secular business. He obeyed, discharged his men, sold his goods, parted with his house. From that time, he not only preached, but was employed in places of the greatest trust. *Journal, Vol. 2, p. 75*

7

The Lord's Supper

❖— *Scripture Sentence*

They devoted themselves to the apostles' teaching and fellowship, to the breaking of bread and the prayers. *Acts 2:42*

❖— *Scripture Readings*

Luke 22:1-13   1 Corinthians 11:17-34
John 13:1-20   *John 6:25-40
Luke 22:14-30   Mark 14:12-25
1 Corinthians 10:14-22

❖— *Silence for Meditation*

❖— *Spiritual Reading*

❖— *Recording Insights and Commitments*

❖— *Prayers of Thanks, Intercession, Petition, and Praise*

❖— *Hymn Portion*

Come, sinners, to the gospel feast, let every soul be Jesus' guest. Ye need not one be left behind, for God hath bid all humankind. *UMH #616*

❖— *Offering All of Life to God*

❖— *Closing Affirmation*

We believe the Lord's Supper is a representation of our redemption, a memorial of the sufferings and death of Christ, and a token of love and union which Christians have with one another. *The Book of Discipline of the United Methodist Church 1996, p. 66*

———— Reflections ————

Much of the population of the world lives in a daily struggle for survival. Scarcity of the elementary needs for life is a daily reality. It is difficult for the poor to believe that anyone knows their plight or cares about their pain. And it is difficult for the affluent to place themselves in a position where they can understand, care about, and respond in meaningful ways to the plight of the poor.

So often affluent and poor are kept separated by our institutions, employment, place of living, and social structure—a social structure that often flows from and contributes to these places of segregation. However, there is one place where everyone is *absolutely* equal, a place where all class, social, racial, economic, educational and every other distinction evaporates as a morning mist under a bright summer sun. That place of absolute equality is at the Lord's Table. Here, as at no other place, we realize our oneness with Christ and our oneness with each other.

Each person stands on equal ground; none is higher or lower. We all come incomplete and broken, we all come seeking wholeness and healing. We all come needy and with empty hands. And soon or late we all realize that only God can mend us, heal us, redeem us, and feed us on the bread of life. This table says little and cares less about what we have done or are doing. Primarily this table testifies to what God has done and is doing.

There are many places where each one of us is excluded. The Table of the Lord is one place where all are included. Everyone is invited and welcomed to this table. Our social structure is often built on distinction that gives and takes power. The Lord's Supper is built on our oneness with Christ and with one another. At this table power flows equally to all; none is excluded, and none need go away empty.

Here we speak not of what we have accomplished, but of what God has accomplished through the life, death and resurrection of Jesus Christ. At this table we are reconciled to God, to neighbor, and even within ourselves. Here we are all offered the gifts of God's redemption and peace, gifts that we have not earned and never can earn in the future. Here we are offered the incomprehensible, communion with God. At this table our hunger for God can be satisfied, our yearning for holiness directed, our purpose for life clarified, and our vision of the meaning of life made clear.

Because all of this is true, the Lord's Supper is a remarkable sign of the reign of God. Here we have a glimpse into what God intends for all humanity. And yet we confess that God's intention is often far from the reality we experience. Unfortunately, even the Lord's Table can be profaned. One of our readings this week reveals the chasm between what God intends and what is practiced (1 Cor. 11). Christians then and now sometimes forget where they are and who is serving as host. And yet, the promise and vision of God's reign is supremely found at this table.

I grew up on a North Dakota farm in the midst of the depression. There was little money, but because of wise, industrious, and loving parents, a deep well, a carefully watered garden, and every kind of animal, there was always enough to eat. My mother made certain that each child received what he needed. The food was simple but nourishing and there was always enough to satisfy the needs of each and of all; we never ran out.

At the Lord's Table there is enough for all. No matter how broken, hungry, or needy I am, there is always enough of the bread of life for me. And my need does not prevent another's need from being recognized and met. No one is shortchanged or denied what is needed. My great need does not jeopardize the resources for my sister or brother. At the Lord's Table there is enough for all.

Our social distinctions fall away at this table, and we begin to see each other as sisters and brothers. When we do, there is awakened within us a desire for a fair share of the goodness of creation for each of God's children. We go from this table determined that the equality and plenty that we experience at the Lord's Table will be the vision toward which we strive in everyday life in the world. Our daily lives are enriched and ordered by the nourishment we receive, for at this table we not only confess with sorrow our sins and receive God's forgiveness and restoration, but we also have renewed our vision of how we are to live in relationship to God and to neighbor.

It is not surprising that Wesley encouraged people to take Communion at least once every week and that he received this gift for himself with even greater frequency. It was for him a constant source of nourishment, healing, and direction. It can be as much for us.

——— *Spiritual Reading* ———

But the sense of it is undeniably found in Scripture. For God hath in Scripture ordained prayer, reading or hearing, and the receiving the Lord's Supper, as the ordinary means of conveying his grace to man. *Journal, Vol. 1, p. 278*

We allow, likewise, that all outward means whatever, if separate from the Spirit of God, cannot profit at all, cannot conduce, in any degree, either to the knowledge or love of God. Without controversy, the help that is done upon earth, He doeth it himself. It is He alone who, by his own almighty power, worketh in us what is pleasing in his sight; and all outward things, unless He work in them and by them, are mere weak and beggarly elements. Whosoever, therefore, imagines there is any intrinsic power in any means whatsoever, does greatly err, not knowing the Scriptures, neither the power of God. We know that there is no inherent power in the words that are spoken in prayer, in the letter of Scripture read, the sound thereof heard, or the bread and wine received in the Lord's Supper; but that it is God alone who is the Giver of every good gift, the Author of all grace; that the whole power is of Him, whereby, through any of these, there is any blessing conveyed to our souls. *Sermon 16, The Means of Grace, Vol. 5, p. 188*

While I was here, I talked largely with a pious woman, whom I could not well understand. I could not doubt of her being quite sincere, nay, and much devoted to God: But she had fallen among some well-meaning enthusiasts, who taught her so to attend to the inward voice, as to quit the society, the preaching, the Lord's Supper, and almost all outward means. I find no persons harder to deal with than these. One knows not how to advise them. They must not act contrary to their conscience, though it be an erroneous one. And who can convince them that it is erroneous? None but the Almighty. *Journal, Vol. 4, p. 78*

I buried the body of Esther Grimaldi, who died in the full triumph of faith. "A mother in Israel" hast thou been; and thy "works shall praise thee in the gates!" During the twelve festival days, we had the Lord's Supper daily; a little emblem of the Primitive Church. May we be followers of them in all things, as they were of Christ! *Journal, Vol. 4, p. 38*

Four of Miss Owen's children desired leave to partake of the Lord's Supper. I talked with them severally, and found they were all still rejoicing in the love of God. And they confirmed the account, that there was only one of their whole number who was unaffected on Monday: But all the rest could then say with confidence, "Lord, thou knowest that I love thee." I suppose such a visitation of children has not been known in England these hundred years. In so marvellous a manner, "out of the mouths of babes and sucklings" God has "perfected praise!" *Journal, Vol. 3, p. 507*

I preached at eight on Southernay-Green, to an extremely quiet congregation. At the cathedral we had an useful sermon, and the whole service was performed with great seriousness and decency. Such an organ I never saw or heard before, so large, beautiful, and so finely toned; and the music of "Glory be to God in the highest," I think exceeded the Messiah itself. I was well pleased to partake of the Lord's Supper with my old opponent, Bishop Lavington. O may we sit down together in the kingdom of our Father! *Journal, Vol. 3, p. 111*

Many were comforted and strengthened both at the Lord's Supper, and at the evening service. I think all jealousies and misunderstandings are now vanished, and the whole society is well knit together. How long will they continue so, considering the unparalleled fickleness of the people in these parts? That God knows. However, he does work now, and we rejoice therein. *Journal, Vol. 3, p. 39*

About one I administered the Lord's Supper to a sick person, with a few of our brethren and sisters. Being straitened for time, I used no extemporary prayer at all; yet the power of God was so unusually present, during the whole time, that several knew not how to contain themselves, being quite overwhelmed with joy and love. *Journal, Vol. 2, p. 184*

I showed at large, 1. That the Lord's Supper was ordained by God, to be a means of conveying to men either preventing, or justifying, or sanctifying grace, according to their several necessities. 2. That the persons for whom it was ordained, are all those who know and feel that they want the grace of God, either to restrain them from sin, or to show their sins forgiven, or to renew their souls in the image of God. 3. That inasmuch as we come to his table, not to give him any thing, but to receive whatsoever he sees best for us, there is no previous preparation indispensably necessary, but a desire to receive whatsoever he pleases to give. And, 4. That no fitness is required at the time of communicating, but a sense of our state, of our utter sinfulness and helplessness; everyone who knows he is fit for hell, being just fit to come to Christ, in this as well as all other ways of his appointment. *Journal, Vol. 1, p. 280*

Wesley's discussions of the various means of grace reveal no consistent hierarchy. They each play valuable roles in the overall task of nurturing Christian holiness. This admitted, he clearly had a particular appreciation for the contribution of the Lord's Supper to this end. He referred to it as the "grand channel" whereby the grace of the Spirit is conveyed to human souls, and identified partaking communion as the first step in working out our salvation. His personal practice conformed to this valuation. He communed every week if possible (a rarity in his day), and often communed daily in the octave of Easter and the twelve festival days of Christmas. As a result he averaged communing about once every five days through his adult life. This helps explain why he encouraged the American Methodists in 1784 to celebrate the Lord's Supper weekly, and published a sermon for all his people in 1787 on "The Duty of Constant Communion." *Randy L. Maddox, Responsible Grace, p. 202*

A good place to start is with the medieval Western suggestion that the mass is a repeated sacrifice for recurrent sin. Wesley appropriated Protestant rejections of this notion, describing the Lord's Supper instead as a commemoration of Christ's sacrifice. However, he meant more by "commemoration" than merely a reminder or memorial .... the point of the Atonement for Wesley was that in Christ's sacrifice we are *convinced* of the love of God for us. Celebration of the Lord's Supper is a primary way in which this conviction is initially sparked and recurrently nurtured. To use language which eucharistic theology has favored in recent years, the communion service "re-presents" Christ's once-for-all sacrifice in dramatic display, conveying its salvific power.

The mention of saving power brings us to a second traditional issue: What does reception of the eucharist do for the believer? On this issue, the Wesleys stood firmly with their Anglican tradition, insisting that the Lord's Supper was truly a *sacrament* that conveys to believers the gracious gift of Christ. To quote Charles, "Ah, tell us no more the spirit and power of Jesus our God is not to be found in this life-giving food." As we have noted repeatedly, this "life-giving food" would provide not only pardon but also empowerment for our growth in Christian holiness. *Randy L. Maddox, Responsible Grace, p. 203*

Actually, the more important contribution that Wesley's mother may have made was to suggest an emphasis on the agency of Holy Spirit as the means by which Christ is present to faithful communicants. At the time, the early Wesley was content simply to affirm that Christ's divinity is united with believers in communion. As his equation of grace with the Presence of the Holy Spirit (and correlated support of the *epiclesis*) matured, he more frequently specified that it was through the Spirit that Christ's benefits are present to faithful participants in the communion service. Thereby he reinforced the "uncreated" nature of sacramental grace—what we encounter in communion is not the static presence of a "benefit" but the pardoning and empowering Presence of a "Person."

A direct implication of the personal quality of eucharistic grace is its co-operant nature—the Spirit (i.e., grace) is always present in the means, but we must responsively welcome this Presence for it to be effective in healing our lives. Full response in such a personal setting is rarely instantaneous, it grows through continuing relationship. Likewise, the healing which our sin-distorted lives require is a long-term project. This is precisely why Wesley encouraged frequent communion! Believers find in each new meal a fresh and deeper encounter with God's empowering love. *Randy L. Maddox, Responsible Grace, p. 204*

8

Reaching Out to the Poor

❖— *Scripture Sentence*
    You shall not strip your vineyard bare, or gather the
    fallen grapes of your vineyard; you shall leave them
    for the poor and the alien: I am the Lord your God.
    Leviticus 19:10

❖— *Scripture Readings*

> Matthew 11:1-15   *James 2:1-7
> Amos 8:4-10   2 Corinthians 8:8-15
> Matthew 19:16-22   Luke 14:1-14
> Luke 6:17-26

❖— *Silence for Meditation*

❖— *Spiritual Reading*

❖— *Recording of Insights and Commitments*

❖— *Prayers of Thanks, Intercession, Petition and Praise*

❖— *Hymn Portion*
    A widow on the poor bestow'd, full of good works,
    divinely good, (works in the Spirit of Jesus done, in
    faith & love to Christ alone) who not on them, but
    Christ, relies, she lays up treasure in the skies. *The
    Unpublished Poetry of Charles Wesley, Vol. II, p. 332*

❖— *Offering All of Life to God*

❖— *Closing Affirmation*
    And God is able to provide you with every blessing
    in abundance, so that by always having enough of
    everything, you may share abundantly in every good
    work. As it is written, "He scatters abroad, he gives
    to the poor; his righteousness endures forever."
    2 Corinthians 9:8-9

———— Reflections ————

One of the few things John Wesley feared was the accumulation of wealth. As a biblical scholar and a practical theologian he was convinced that to follow Jesus Christ meant involvement with, and ministry among and to, the poor. This conviction led him to live on a modest income even when his writing was producing significant return. His solution was to give away all but the money he needed to buy the essentials.

This understanding of the relationship between following Christ and involvement with the poor led him to some unusual practices. It was not uncommon for him to beg in order to raise money for the poor. His journal entry for January 4th, 1785 reads in part:

> So on this, and the four following days, I walked through the town, and begged two hundred pounds, in order to clothe them that needed it most. But it was hard work, as most of the streets were filled with melting snow, which often lay ankle deep: so that my feet were steeped in snow water nearly from morning till evening.

Not only did Wesley beg on behalf of the poor, he preached to them and found ways to be with them. His journal is filled with entries that describe his experiences of visiting the poor, the prisoner, the sorrowing and the suffering. The false stereotypes of the day were shattered as he came to work with and to know the poor and needy of the world. Had he ignored God's urging to ministry with the poor he would have missed a large segment of the population that turned toward Christ through the Methodist movement. He would also have missed living and witnessing to a balanced faith that emphasized love for God and love for neighbor in very simple and practical ways.

Another way that Wesley sought to relate to the poor was through his decision to publish inexpensive Christian resources. He wanted every person to have access to the gospel and the simple, practical, and profound teaching that the gospel had inspired. Always an evangelist, he wanted every person to have equal access to the gifts of God that came through an enlightened and growing faith.

Gifted scholar and preacher that he was, John Wesley could have ignored the poor and had a fruitful ministry with persons in the middle and upper middle class. But he chose to relate to all, especially those with special needs.

Prisoners, the sick, orphans, widows, the poor, and all who suffered received his care because he believed them to be special recipients of God's care. He was certain that if God was God of all, then no follower of God could turn away from the pain, suffering, or need of any of God's children. It was this practical side of his experiential theology that became the driving force of the social revolution that followed wherever the Methodist revival took hold.

In a world where the chasm between rich and poor is growing at an alarming rate, the Methodist model is both promising and threatening. It is promising in that here is an answer to the incredible suffering of the poor in our land and around the world. It is threatening because no one can escape responsibility for the needs of another. In Wesley's view we are our brothers' keeper, and as long as there is one person in need, no Christian can rest content.

The early Methodists were trained to see the needy and they were taught how to respond. It was the expected way of life for a Methodist. To become a part of this movement was to throw one's life with almost reckless abandon into the battle for justice and equal opportunity for all of God's children.

Could it be that the Methodist movement has been preserved for such a moment as this? We live in a time when much of the secular world and much of the religious world has turned its back on the pain and suffering of the least and the lost. We have developed a certain immunity and blindness to the enormous suffering of the world. And yet, such a time as this provides tremendous opportunity for all who seek to faithfully follow Jesus Christ. The person who can see the face of Christ in every needy person in the world (Matt. 25) is surely on the high road of faithfulness.

How is it with Methodism or Christianity as you know it? Is there consuming passion for the poor, the needy, the prisoner, the sick? A passion that is second only to love for God? If the answer is yes, how can this passion be shared with others? If the answer is no, what needs to happen to lead Methodism and Christianity to this level of faithfulness? This may also be a good time for some personal examination. What are you and I willing to do and be in order to awaken a passion for and ministry with the poor? To answer wisely is to place ourselves clearly on a journey of faithfulness that leads to life abundant and eternal within the Kingdom of God. What a wonderful place to live!

Spiritual Reading

He [John Fletcher] frequently said he was never happier than when he had given away the last penny he had in his house. If at any time I had gold in my drawers, it seemed to afford him no comfort. But if he could find a handful of small silver, when he was going out to see the sick, he would express as much pleasure over it as a miser would in discovering a bag of hid treasure. He was never better pleased with my employment, than when he had set me to prepare food or physic for the poor. He was hardly able to relish his dinner, if some sick neighbour had not a part of it; and sometimes, if any one of them was in want, I could not keep the linen in his drawers. On Sundays he provided for numbers of people who came from a distance to hear the word; and his house, as well as his heart, was devoted to their convenience: To relieve them that were afflicted in body or mind was the delight of his heart. Once a poor man, who feared God, being brought into great difficulties, he took down all the pewter from the kitchen shelves, saying, "This will help you; and I can do without it. A wooden trencher will serve me just as well." In epidemic and contagious distempers, when the neighbours were afraid to nurse the sick, he has gone from house to house, seeking some that were willing to undertake it. And when none could be found, he has offered his service, to sit up with them himself. *The Life and Death of the Reverend John Fletcher, Vol. 11, p. 346*

But I will not talk of giving to God, or leaving, half your fortune. You might think this to be too high a price for heaven. I will come to lower terms. Are there not a few among you that could give a hundred pounds, perhaps some that could give a thousand, and yet leave your children as much as would help them to work out their own salvation? With two thousand pounds, and not much less, we could supply the present wants of all our poor, and put them in a way of supplying their own wants for the time to come. Now, suppose this could be done, are we clear before God while it is not done? Is not the neglect of it one cause why so many are still sick and weak among you; and that both in soul and in body? that they still grieve the Holy Spirit, by preferring the fashions of the world to the commands of God? And I many times doubt whether we Preachers are not, in some measure, partakers of their sin. I am in doubt whether it is not a kind of partiality. I doubt whether it is not a great sin to keep them in our society. May it not hurt their souls, by encouraging them to persevere in walking contrary to the Bible? And may it not, in some measure, intercept the salutary influences of the blessed Spirit upon the whole community? *Sermon 116, Causes of the Inefficacy of Christianity, Vol. 7, p. 287*

At Epworth in Lincolnshire, the town where I was born, a beggar came to a house in the market place, and begged a morsel of bread, saying she was very hungry. The master bid her begone. . . . She called at a second, and begged a little small beer, saying she was very thirsty. She had much the same answer. At a third door she begged a little water; saying she was very faint. But this man also was too conscientious to encourage common beggars. The boys, seeing a ragged creature turned from door to door, began to pelt her with snow-balls. She looked up, lay down, and died! Would you wish to be the man who refused that poor wretch a morsel of bread or a cup of water? *Sermon 112, The Rich Man and Lazarus, Vol. 7, p. 150*

Two-and-forty years ago, having a desire to furnish poor people with cheaper, shorter, and plainer books than any I had seen, I wrote many small tracts, generally a penny a-piece; and afterwards several larger. Some of these had such a sale as I never thought of; and, by this means, I unawares became rich. But I never desired or endeavoured after it. And now that it is come upon me unawares, I lay up no treasures upon earth; I lay up nothing at all. My desire and endeavour, in this respect, is, to "wind my bottom round the year." I cannot help leaving my books behind me whenever God calls me hence; but, in every other respect, my own hands will be my executors. *Sermon 87, The Danger of Riches, Vol. 7, p. 9*

Dear Sir, I know what you feel for the poor, and I also sympathize with you. Here is a hard season coming on, and everything very dear; thousands of poor souls, yea,

Christians, dread the approaching calamities. O that God would stir up the hearts of all that believe themselves his children, to evidence it by showing mercy to the poor, as God has shown them mercy! Surely the real children of God will do it of themselves; for it is the natural fruit of a branch in Christ. I would not desire them to lose one meal in a week, but to use as cheap food, clothes ... as possible. *Journal, Vol. 3, p. 307*

I thought proper to send you a few lines concerning what you spoke of last night. How good it was that you put us all together as one family; that each might do his utmost to help all his brethren! Had you spoke of this sooner, and opened your mind as freely as you did yesterday, where I have given one shilling, I would have given one pound. My heart was rejoiced at the good news, so as my tongue cannot express. I was ready to cry out, with Zaccheus, "Lo, the half of my goods I give to the poor." I have sent you two guineas towards carrying on the work of the Lord. And may the blessing of the Lord go with it; for I give it freely; I would rather it had been twoscore. *Journal, Vol. 3, p. 245*

Among the letters I read in public last week, was one from Mr. Gillies, giving an account of a society lately formed at Glasgow, for promoting Christian Knowledge among the poor, chiefly by distributing Bibles among them, and other religious books. I could not then help expressing my amazement, that nothing of this kind had been attempted in Ireland; and inquiring if it was not high time that such a society should be formed in Dublin. This morning Dr. Tisdale showed me a paper, which the Archbishop had just sent to each of his Clergy; exhorting them to erect a society for the distribution of books among the poor. Thanks be to God for this! Whether we or they, it is all one, so God be known, loved, and obeyed. *Journal, Vol. 2, p. 439*

Wesley was, if nothing else, the theologian of experience. This did not mean for him a concentration upon isolated moments of interior religious excitement, but rather the immersion in lived experience, in the texture and duration of sensory involvement. If you want to know what love is, you live the life of love and reflect on the vicissitudes of this journey through time. Similarly, if one is to know something of poverty one must spend the time and energy to be with the poor and to appropriate what is encountered there.

It is in this light that we can understand the importance for Wesley of "visiting" the sick, the poor, the imprisoned. Apart from this practice of visitation, no real experience of the plight of the poor is possible. Without it, the nerve of compassion is cut and the possibility of a pertinent and transforming praxis is lost.

The practice of visiting the destitute and marginalized of English society was a feature of Wesley's own Methodist discipline from the early days at Oxford until the end of his long career. Wesley's early motivation may have been simply to obey what, on the basis of Matthew 25, he took to be a clear command of the gospel. In his view, this would seem to be adequate motivation for anyone. . . .

However, Wesley realized that there were additional, and no less weighty, reasons for this practice than the sheer force of dominical authority. Thus he could remark that it was far better "to *carry* relief to the poor, than to send it," not only for their sake but also because this was "far more apt to soften our heart, and to make us naturally care for each other" (*Journal,* November 24, 1760, III:28). This last point is reinforced by Wesley when he adds that this visitation may also serve as a means of "increasing your sympathy with the afflicted, your benevolence, and all social affections" ("On Visiting the Sick," VII:119). Without this sort of personal engagement "you could not gain that increase in lowliness, in patience, in tenderness of spirit, in sympathy with the afflicted, which you might have gained, if you had assisted them in person" (Ibid., VII:120). Thus the practice of visitation was directly necessary for developing the sort of compassion that, for Wesley, was the heart of true religion.

Indeed, Wesley could even maintain that visiting the poor and sick and imprisoned was a means of grace, to be ranked alongside private and public prayer or the sacraments themselves ("On Zeal," VII:60). Thus Wesley said of visiting those whom today we would call the marginalized: "The walking herein is essentially necessary, as to the continuance of that faith wherein we are already saved by grace, so to the attainment of everlasting salvation" ("On

Visiting the Sick," VII:117). *Theodore W. Jennings Jr., Good News to the Poor, pp. 53–54*

The value, then, of visiting the poor is that both hearts and minds may be transformed, that experience may lead to understanding.

The stereotype that Wesley explodes here and throughout his *Journal* is that of the laziness of the poor. Then as now there were those who shrugged off the plight of the poor and even made the poor culpable of their poverty with the smug assertion that the poor are indigent because they are indolent. Neither then or now could such a generalization survive any acquaintance with the poor themselves. This blindness can only be cured by the sort of concrete experience with the poor that Wesley insisted on as part of Methodist discipline in his own day. Only in this way is it possible to experience the transformation of heart and mind that comes of visiting the poor.

With a change of heart and mind comes the possibility of action. It is then possible to speak out on behalf of the marginalized, as Wesley does when he speaks of the horrors of poverty or attacks the "devilishly false" bromide that the poor are lazy. This leads to a call for the transformation of others in their attitudes and behavior.

The result of this visiting, finally, is an appropriate action aimed at aiding the poor. Thus Wesley writes again, "On the following days, I visited many of our poor, to see with my own eyes what their wants were, and how they might be effectually relieved" (*Journal*, Feb. 13, 1785, IV: 296; see also Feb. 8, 1787, IV: 358). *Theodore W. Jennings Jr., Good News to the Poor, pp. 55–56*

9

Marks of a Methodist

❖— *Scripture Sentence*
For by grace you have been saved through faith, and this is not your own doing; it is the gift of God. *Ephesians 2:8*

❖— *Scripture Readings*

John 3:16-21	Revelation 7:9-17
John 3:22-30	Romans 13:8-14
2 Corinthians 6:1-10	Jude 17–25
*Philippians 2:12-18	

❖— *Silence for Meditation*

❖— *Spiritual Reading*

❖— *Recording Insights and Commitments*

❖— *Prayers of Thanks, Intercession, Petition, and Praise*

❖— *Hymn Portion*
Thy mighty name salvation is, and keeps my happy soul above; comfort it brings, and power and peace, and joy and everlasting love; to me with thy dear name are given pardon and holiness and heaven. *UMH #153*

❖— *Offering All of Life to God*

❖— *Closing Affirmation*
For we are what he has made us, created in Christ Jesus for good works, which God prepared beforehand to be our way of life. *Ephesians 2:10*

——— Reflections ———

We were in a small village in The People's Republic of China where our bus stopped for lunch. With about thirty other western tourists, my wife and I walked toward a small shopping area. Almost instantly we were followed by children and adults who carefully observed our clothing, our walk, and were not embarrassed to get very close for a better look. In some ways it was unsettling and in others amusing. But it was clear that we could not hide. *Western* was written all over us and no matter how hard we tried to blend in, it was clear that we were *different*.

John Wesley believed that Methodists should be as difficult to hide as visitors in a foreign land. It was his conviction that authentic Christianity carried with it some distinguishing characteristics that would set Christians apart from the rest of society. There was no desire to be different for the sake of difference. However, there was the strong conviction that one who followed the way of Jesus Christ would be seen as different in a world that followed its own way. Thus the ridicule of the disciplined "Methodists" was seen not as condemnation of error but as affirmation of truth.

Wesley believed right theology was important, especially in one's core beliefs. The difference he sought in Methodists was the living out of that theology in everyday life. He believed that when these core beliefs were in place and guiding all of life there would be noticeable results. These noticeable results were the marks of a Methodist. Those characteristics set Methodists apart from the rest of Christendom and the culture of the age.

Methodists today live in a world that seeks to press everyone into its own mold. We are encouraged not to make waves and we are discouraged from being too "radical" in our life of faith, lest we be labeled as fanatics. And if we listen to the voice of the culture around us it is quite easy to hide, to be absorbed into the mainstream of life that flows all around us. There are benefits to being assimilated into the mainstream, to being unnoticed. We may get along more easily with those around us; we may even feel less stress in our work place. But are these benefits greater than the value of walking faithfully with Jesus Christ in all of life? I think the answer for each of us is clear.

How then do we live so that others will immediately

know that we as Methodists are following Jesus Christ in unquestioned obedience? First of all, we live in the power, presence, and peace of Jesus Christ. We do not attempt to follow the road of faithfulness on our own. We recognize our weakness and take every opportunity to be strengthened and guided by God. While our efforts are required, this is not a self-help project. It is rather a faith project, faith in the One who made us and who alone can sustain us.

The marks of a Methodist are seen in a life that is clearly offered to God with an unqualified commitment. When this happens life is transformed and begins to bear the characteristics of the One who is being followed. To live with God and to walk with Jesus Christ profoundly shapes and transforms the individual life. To intentionally be in God's presence—to listen, learn, and obey—is to be transformed. Our ideas are molded, our plans are adjusted, and our dreams are shaped as we willingly and intentionally live in the presence of God.

When we walk in companionship with Jesus Christ we begin to think and to act like Jesus. It is impossible to live in close communion with any person and not take on some of the qualities of that person. So it is with Jesus Christ. To live with Jesus is to begin to take on the qualities that marked his life. Unqualified love for and obedience to God, unconditional love of neighbor and a radical selflessness were an integral part of the life and ministry of Jesus. To follow Jesus is to incorporate these qualities into our lives as well. And to do so is to begin to bear the mark of a Methodist that John Wesley sought to see implanted in everyone who followed the Methodist way.

As we read and reflect on the marks that Wesley identified, it is appropriate to consider how we could incorporate these qualities more fully into our own lives. What would we need to change? What would we need to strengthen? What kind of help would we need to live such an authentic Christian life that others would immediately know that we belong to God? The answers to our inquiries could lead to frequent comments such as, "I see you are a Methodist Christian." It would be a worthy mark to bear.

"What then is the mark? Who is a Methodist, according to your own account?" I answer: A Methodist is one who has "the love of God shed abroad in his heart by the Holy Ghost given unto him;" one who "loves the Lord his God with all his heart, and with all his soul, and with all his mind, and with all his strength." God is the joy of his heart, and the desire of his soul; which is constantly crying out, "Whom have I in heaven but thee? And there is none upon earth that I desire beside thee! My God and my all! Thou art the strength of my heart, and my portion for ever!"

He is therefore happy in God, yea, always happy, as having in him "a well of water springing up into everlasting life," and overflowing his soul with peace and joy. "Perfect love" having now "cast out fear," he "rejoices evermore." He "rejoices in the Lord always," even "in God his Saviour;" and in the Father, "through our Lord Jesus Christ, by whom he hath now received the atonement." "Having" found "redemption through his blood, the forgiveness of his sins," he cannot but rejoice, whenever he looks back on the horrible pit out of which he is delivered; when he sees "all his transgressions blotted out as a cloud, and his iniquities as a thick cloud." He cannot but rejoice, whenever he looks on the state wherein he now is; "being justified freely, and having peace with God through our Lord Jesus Christ." For "he that believeth, hath the witness" of this "in himself;" being now the son of God by faith. "Because he is a son, God hath sent forth the Spirit of his Son into his heart, crying, Abba, Father!" And "the Spirit itself beareth witness with his spirit, that he is a child of God." He rejoiceth also, whenever he looks forward, "in hope of the glory that shall be revealed;" yea, this his joy is full, and all his bones cry out, "Blessed be the God and Father of our Lord Jesus Christ, who, according to his abundant mercy, hath begotten me again to a living hope—of an inheritance incorruptible, undefiled, and that fadeth not away, reserved in heaven for me!"

And he who hath this hope, thus "full of immortality in everything giveth thanks;" as knowing that this (whatsoever it is) "is the will of God in Christ Jesus concerning him." From him, therefore, he cheerfully receives all, saying, "Good is the will of the Lord;" and whether the Lord giveth or taketh away, equally "blessing the name of the Lord."

For he hath "learned, in whatsoever state he is, therewith to be content." He knoweth "both how to be abased and how to abound. Everywhere and in all things he is instructed both to be full and to be hungry, both to abound and suffer need." Whether in ease or pain, whether in sickness or health, whether in life or death, he giveth thanks from the ground of his heart to Him who orders it for good; knowing that as "every good gift cometh from above," so none but good can come from the Father of Lights, into whose hand he has wholly committed his body and soul, as into the hands of a faithful Creator. He is therefore "careful" (anxiously or uneasily) "for nothing;" as having "cast all his care on Him that careth for him," and "in all things" resting on him, after "making his request known to him with thanksgiving."

For indeed he "prays without ceasing." It is given him "always to pray and not to faint." Not that he is always in the house of prayer; though he neglects no opportunity of being there. Neither is he always on his knees, although he often is, or on his face, before the Lord his God. Nor yet is he always crying aloud to God, or calling upon him in words: For many times "the Spirit maketh intercession for him with groans that cannot be uttered." But at all times the language of his heart is this: "Thou brightness of the eternal glory, unto thee is my heart, though without a voice, and my silence speaketh unto thee." And this is true prayer, and this alone. But his heart is ever lifted up to God, at all times and in all places. In this he is never hindered, much less interrupted, by any person or thing. In retirement or company, in leisure, business, or conversation, his heart is ever with the Lord. Whether he lie down or rise up, God is in all his thoughts; he walks with God continually, having the loving eye of his mind still fixed upon him, and everywhere "seeing Him that is invisible."

And while he thus always exercises his love to God, by praying without ceasing, rejoicing evermore, and in everything giving thanks, this commandment is written in his heart, "That he who loveth God, love his brother also." And he accordingly loves his neighbour as himself; he loves every man as his own soul. His heart is full of love to all mankind, to every child of "the Father of the spirits of all flesh." That a man is not personally known to him, is no bar to his love; no, nor that he is known to be such as he approves not, that he repays hatred for his good-will. For he "loves his enemies;" yea, and the enemies of God, "the evil and the unthankful." And if it be not in his power to "do good to them that hate him," yet he ceases not to pray for them, though they continue to spurn his love, and still "despitefully use him and persecute him."

For he is "pure in heart." The love of God has purified his heart from all revengeful passions, from envy, malice, and wrath, from every unkind temper or malign affection. It hath cleansed him from pride and haughtiness of spirit, whereof alone cometh contention. And he hath now "put on bowels of mercies, kindness, humbleness of mind, meekness, longsuffering:" So that he "forbears and forgives, if he had a quarrel against any; even as God in Christ hath forgiven him." And indeed all possible ground for contention, on his part, is utterly cut off. For none can take from him what he desires; seeing he "loves not the world, nor" any of "the things of the world;" being now "crucified to the world, and the world crucified to him;" being dead to all that is in the world, both to "the lust of the flesh, the lust of the eye, and the pride of life." For all his desire is unto God, and to the remembrance of his name.

Agreeable to this his one desire, is the one design of his life, namely, "not to do his own will, but the will of Him that sent him." His one intention at all times and in all things is, not to please himself, but Him whom his soul loveth. He has a single eye. And because "his eye is single, his whole body is full of light." Indeed, where the loving eye of the soul is continually fixed upon God, there can be no darkness at all, "but the whole is light; as when the bright shining of a candle doth enlighten the house." God then reigns alone. All that is in the soul is holiness to the Lord. There is not a motion in his heart, but is according to his will. Every thought that arises points to Him, and is in obedience to the law of Christ.

And the tree is known by its fruits. For as he loves God, so he keeps his commandments; not only some, or most of them, but all, from the least to the greatest. He is not content to "keep the whole law, and offend in one point;" but has, in all points, "a conscience void of offence towards God and towards man." Whatever God has forbidden, he avoids; whatever God hath enjoined, he doeth; and that whether it be little or great, hard or easy, joyous or grievous to the flesh. He "runs the way of God's commandments," now he hath his heart set at liberty. It is his glory so to do; it is his daily crown of rejoicing, "to do the will of God on earth, as it is done in heaven;" knowing it is the highest privilege of "the angels of God, of those that excel in strength, to fulfil his commandments, and to hearken to the voice of his word."

All the commandments of God he accordingly keeps, and that with all his might. For his obedience is in proportion to his love, the source from whence it flows. And therefore, loving God with all his heart, he serves him with all his strength. He continually presents his soul and body a living sacrifice, holy, acceptable to God; entirely and without reserve devoting himself, all he has, and all he is, to his glory. All the talents he has received, he constantly employs according to his Master's will; every power and faculty of his soul, every member of his body. Once he "yielded" them "unto sin" and the devil, "as instruments of unrighteousness;" but now, "being alive from the dead, he yields" them all "as instruments of righteousness unto God."

By consequence, whatsoever he doeth, it is all to the glory of God. In all his employments of every kind, he not only aims at this, (which is implied in having a single eye,) but actually attains it. His business and refreshments, as well as his prayers, all serve this great end. Whether he sit in his house or walk by the way, whether he lie down or rise up, he is promoting, in all he speaks or does, the one business of his life; whether he put on his apparel, or labour, or eat or drink, or divert himself from too wasting labour, it all tends to advance the glory of God, by peace and good-will among men. His one invariable rule is this, "Whatsoever ye do, in word or deed, do it all in the name of the Lord Jesus, giving thanks to God and the Father by him."

Nor do the customs of the world at all hinder his "running the race that is set before him." He knows that vice does not lose its nature, though it becomes ever so fashionable; and remembers, that "every man is to give an account of himself to God." He cannot, therefore, "follow" even "a multitude to do evil." He cannot "fare sumptuously every day," or "make provision for the flesh to fulfil the lusts thereof." He cannot "lay up treasures upon earth," any more than he can take fire into his bosom. He cannot "adorn himself," on any pretence, "with gold or costly apparel." He cannot join in or countenance any diversion which has the least tendency to vice of any kind. He cannot "speak evil" of his neighbour, any more than he can lie either for God or man. He cannot utter an unkind word of any one; for love keeps the door of his lips. He cannot speak "idle words;" "no corrupt communication" ever "comes out of his mouth," as is all that "which is" not "good to the use of edifying," not "fit to minister grace to the hearers." But "whatsoever things are pure, whatsoever things are lovely, whatsoever things are" justly "of good report," he thinks and speaks, and acts, "adorning the Gospel of our Lord Jesus Christ in all things."

Lastly. As he has time, he "does good unto all men;" unto neighbours and strangers, friends and enemies: And that in every possible kind; not only to their bodies, by "feeding the hungry, clothing the naked, visiting those that are sick or in prison;" but much more does he labour to do good to their souls, as of the ability which God giveth; to awaken those that sleep in death; to bring those who are awakened to the atoning blood, that, "being justified by faith, they may have peace with God;" and to provoke those who have peace with God to abound more in love and in good works. And he is willing to "spend and be spent herein," even "to be offered up on the sacrifice and service of their faith," so they may "all come unto the measure of the stature of the fulness of Christ."

These are the principles and practices of our sect; these are the marks of a true Methodist. By these alone do those who are in derision so called, desire to be distinguished from other men. If any man say, "Why, these are only the common fundamental principles of Christianity!" thou hast said; so I mean; this is the very truth; I know they are no other; and I would to God both thou and all men knew, that I, and all who follow my judgment, do vehemently refuse to be distinguished from other men, by any but the common principles of Christianity,—the plain, old Christianity that I teach, renouncing and detesting all other marks of distinction. *The Character of a Methodist, Vol. 8, pp. 341–46*

10

The Centrality of Scripture

❖— *Scripture Sentence*
You search the scriptures, because you think that in them you have eternal life; and it is they that testify on my behalf. *John 5:39*

❖— *Scripture Readings*

Luke 4:16-22	Romans 4:1-8
Acts 17:10-15	*Luke 24:13-27
Mark 12:18-27	Luke 24:28-35
Acts 18:24-28	

❖— *Silence for Meditation*

❖— *Spiritual Reading*

❖— *Recording of Insights and Commitments*

❖— *Prayers of Thanks, Intercession, Petition, and Praise*

❖— *Hymn Portion*
Come, Holy Ghost (for moved by thee the prophets wrote and spoke), unlock the truth, thyself the key, unseal the sacred book. *UMH #603*

❖— *Offering All of Life to God*

❖— *Closing Affirmation*
All scripture is inspired by God and is useful for teaching, for reproof, for correction, and for training in righteousness, so that everyone who belongs to God may be proficient, equipped for every good work. *2 Timothy 3:16-17*

—— Reflections ——

The Bible continues to be a best seller, and it is prominently displayed in the hands or under the arm of prominent people. Even though our culture is becoming more diverse, the Bible is still tucked away in a drawer in most hotel rooms in the United States.

The perplexing social issues of our time often become the battleground for competing understandings and a variety of uses and misuses of the Bible. Each side can find justification for its position and ammunition to destroy its opponents' position. Every day the Bible is read in formal and informal services of worship around the world and millions of persons turn to it every day for direction, comfort, and hope.

Then why does the influence of the scriptures in our time seem so minimal? Could it be that we do not really accept the Bible as central to our lives? Is it possible that we have not permitted the scriptures to become the guide of our lives and the rule of our actions? The Wesley brothers believed that scripture should be central to all belief and action. Their sermons, letters, and hymns proclaim an almost unparalleled fidelity and obedience to the Bible. Theirs was not a cursory reading and dismissal of the scripture but rather an incorporation of scripture into the very fabric of everyday life.

There is a way to read scripture that goes far beyond mining a text for some golden nugget that will transform an otherwise lifeless sermon. And there is an incorporation of scripture into daily life that is far more responsible than using it as a weapon against an opposing view or as a prop to hold up an uncertain position. It is to ask simply and honestly: "In the light of all I understand of the scripture, what is God saying to me in this text today?"

John Wesley proclaimed the centrality of scripture for doctrine and for holy living. It was the basic authority for the Christian life and where its truths appeared clear there was no alternative but obedience if one desired to be a faithful Christian.

Randy Maddox points out that Wesley approached scripture with his own unique exegetical principles. Wesley believed that the text must be interpreted according to the analogy of faith. According to Maddox this referred to a connected chain of scripture truths. Four of these scripture truths were the corruption of sin, justification by faith, the new birth, and present inward and outward holiness (Maddox, *Responsible Grace*, 38). In other words, scripture truth itself became the interpreting principle. In Wesley's view the four truths identified above were clearly and substantially identified as major themes in the scripture and in life experience.

John Wesley was a competent biblical scholar, reading the Bible in the original languages, and was well trained at Oxford and as a priest in the Church of England. However, he never placed himself above the scripture. He was fearless in his scholarship and yet utterly obedient to the scripture's message for his ministry and for all of life.

Wesley knew that the transformed life was not accidental. He was convinced that one does not drift into inward or outward holiness. God's grace required response and that response included a careful reading, reflection upon, and incorporation of and obedience to scripture in everyday living. God's grace was always available and scripture was one way for Christians to appropriate that grace into daily life.

Do you wish to live a life of inward and outward holiness? Do you desire to live with God in the midst of this broken world? Do you want the assurance and comfort of sins forgiven and guilt removed? Do you desire some guiding principles that can bring direction to your personal and corporate decision making? If the answer is yes to any of these questions, you will want to read and reflect upon the scriptures. For scripture remains the primary source of revelation and authority for those who are descendants of Wesley.

In this book you are encouraged to read the suggested texts for each day as though they were directed specifically to you. Permit the passage to address you, examine you, speak to you, and direct you in this daily companionship with scripture and its Author.

In an age of accelerated change and great uncertainty most of us look for some authority or guiding principle that will not only help us understand what is happening in the world, but will help us to live peacefully, fruitfully, and faithfully as Christians. The scriptures, carefully, prayerfully, and honestly read, can provide that vast resource of wisdom and direction for all of us.

——— Spiritual Reading ———

Would it not be advisable, (1.) To set apart a little time, if you can, every morning and evening for that purpose? (2.) At each time, if you have leisure, to read a chapter out of the Old, and one out of the New, Testament; if you cannot do this, to take a single chapter or a part of one? (3.) To read this with a single eye, to know the whole will of God, and a fixed resolution to do it? In order to know his will, you should (4.) Have a constant eye to the analogy of faith, the connexion and harmony there is between those grand, fundamental doctrines, original sin, justification by faith, the new birth, inward and outward holiness: (5.) Serious and earnest prayer should be constantly used before we consult the oracles of God: seeing "Scripture can only be understood through the same Spirit whereby it was given." Our reading should likewise be closed with prayer, that what we read may be written on our hearts: (6.) It might also be of use, if, while we read, we were frequently to pause, and examine ourselves by what we read, both with regard to our hearts and lives. This would furnish us with matter of praise, where we found God had enabled us to conform to his blessed will; and matter of humiliation and prayer, where we were conscious of having fallen short. And whatever light you then receive should be used to the uttermost, and that immediately. Let there be no delay. Whatever you resolve, begin to execute the first moment you can. So shall you find this word to be indeed the power of God unto present and eternal salvation. *Works Abridged from Various Authors by John Wesley, Vol. 14, p. 253*

Now, the Bible can have no other office or power, than to direct you to Christ. How then can you more magnify the Bible than by going from its teaching, to be taught by Christ? So you set Christ and the Bible in flat opposition to each other! And is this the way we are to learn of him? Nay, but we are taught of him, not by going from the Bible, but by keeping close to it. Both by the Bible and by experience we know, that his word and his Spirit act in connexion with each other. And thus it is, that by Christ continually teaching and strengthening him through the Scripture, "the man of God is made perfect, and thoroughly furnished for every good word and work." *An Extract of a Letter to the Reverend Mr. Law, Vol. 9, p. 505*

What is it you would have us prove by miracles? that the doctrines we preach are true? This is not the way to prove that: We prove the doctrines we preach by Scripture and reason. *A Letter to Mr. Fleury, Vol. 9, p. 186*

You receive not the ancient, but the modern Mystics, as the best interpreters of Scripture: And in conformity to these, you mix much of man's wisdom with the wisdom of God: You greatly refine the plain religion taught by the letter of Holy Writ, and philosophize on almost every part of it, to accommodate it to the Mystic theory. Hence you talk much, in a manner wholly unsupported by Scripture, against mixing nature with grace, against imagination, and concerning the animal spirits, mimicking the power of the Holy Ghost. Hence your brethren zealously caution us against animal joy, against natural love of one another, and against selfish love of God; against which (or any of them) there is no one caution in all the Bible. And they have, in truth, greatly lessened, and had well-nigh destroyed, brother love from among us. *Journal, Vol. 1, p. 330*

Permit me to speak plainly. If by Catholic principles you mean any other than Scriptural, they weigh nothing with me: I allow no other rule, whether of faith or practice, than the Holy Scriptures: But on scriptural principles, I do not think it hard to justify whatever I do. God in Scripture commands me, according to my power, to instruct the ignorant, reform the wicked, confirm the virtuous. Man forbids me to do this in another's parish; that is, in effect, to do it at all; seeing I have now no parish of my own, nor probably ever shall. Whom then shall I hear, God or man? "If it be just to obey man rather than God, judge you. A dispensation of the Gospel is committed to me; and woe is me, if I preach not the Gospel." But where shall I preach it, upon the principles you mention? Why, not in Europe, Asia, Africa, or America; not in any of the Christian parts, at least, of the habitable earth. For all these, after a sort, are divided into parishes. If it be said, "Go back, then, to the Heathens from whence you came:" Nay, but neither could I now (on your principles) preach to them; for all the Heathens in Georgia belong to the parish either of Savannah or Frederica. *Journal, Vol. 1, p. 201*

Many came to me and earnestly advised me not to preach abroad in the afternoon, because there was a combination of several persons, who threatened terrible things. This report being spread abroad, brought many thither of the better sort of people; (so called:) and added, I believe, more than a thousand to the ordinary congregation. The scripture to which, not my choice, but the providence of God, directed me, was, "Fear not thou, for I am with thee; yea, I will uphold thee with the right hand of my righteousness." The power of God came with his word: So that none scoffed, or interrupted, or opened his mouth. *Journal, Vol. 1, p. 198*

John Wesley's guidelines for reading scripture are an excellent description of the posture that is necessary if our reading is to become an encounter with the living, penetrating Word of God. Wesley's guidelines move us from the informational to the formational level of reading, from the functional to the relational dynamic of response to what we read, and from the "doing" to the "being" mode of implementation of what we read.

In introducing his guidelines, Wesley says:

> This is the way to understand [informational] the things of God: "Meditate thereon day and night;" so shall you attain the best knowledge, even to "know the only true God, and Jesus Christ whom He hath sent" [formational/relational]. And this knowledge will lead you "to love Him, because He hath first loved us;" yea, "to love the Lord your God with all your heart, and with all your soul, and with all your mind, and with all your strength" [relational/being].... And in consequence of this, while you joyfully experience all the holy tempers described in this book [being], you will likewise be outwardly "holy as He that hath called you is holy, in all manner of conversation" [doing which flows from being].

Wesley is here speaking of a process of approaching scripture that opens us to the living Word. This approach leads us into spiritual disciplines through which God can break the crust of self which garbles, distorts, and debases us, and which results in the nurture of the Word that enables us to be the word God speaks us forth to be in the world.

If we desire to read scripture in such a way that we become, through the shaping of the Word, the word God speaks us forth to be, the first thing Wesley tells us is, "To set apart a little time, if you can, every morning and every evening for that purpose." I hear Wesley saying two things in this first guideline, which I would commend to you for your own use of scripture in your spiritual formation.

First our use of scripture in spiritual formation must be a regular, consistent, daily feeding upon the Word; it must be a spiritual discipline.... We are to undertake reading scripture as a regular, consistent discipline, an action, a "function," something we "do;" but we offer it up to God as a means of grace so our reading can become formational, relational. This offering is, as we have seen, the heart, the core, the inner dynamic of spiritual discipline. But then, there is also the regularity of the discipline, the persistent, daily sticking with it.

Second, in the words "set apart," I hear Wesley saying there needs to be not only a disciplined, daily time of reading the scripture, but an unhindered time....

Wesley's second instruction is, "At each time, if you have leisure, read a chapter out of the Old and one out of the New Testament; if you cannot do this, take a single chapter, or a part of one." ...

Once you have developed a means of working through scripture in a balanced and formational way, Wesley says that you should approach each passage "with a single eye, to know the whole will of God, and a fixed resolution to do it." This is the heart of the approach to scripture in spiritual formation....

Wesley then says, "Have a constant eye to the analogy of faith, the connection and harmony there is between those grand fundamental doctrines, original sin, justification by faith, the new birth, inward and outward holiness." We must realize that in the scripture we are not dealing with isolated pieces that are somehow hermetically sealed from one another. We are dealing with a great, holistic unity. We are dealing with the living reality of God's purpose, power, and presence in our lives and in our world....

The fifth thing Wesley says about approaching the scripture is that "serious and earnest prayer should be consistently used before we consult the oracles of God; seeing 'Scripture can only be understood through the same Spirit whereby it was given.' Our reading should likewise be closed with prayer, that what we read may be written on our hearts." ...

Finally, Wesley says, "It might also be of use [he is a master of understatement!] if, while, we read, we were frequently to pause and examine ourselves by what we read, both with regard to our heart and lives." This is the conscious, disciplined opening of ourselves to be addressed by the Word. It is, on the one hand, the examination of the outer actions of our lives. What is going on in our personal and corporate relationships? What is taking place in our patterns of reaction and response? What is happening at work, at home, in the church, in our social activities? What is occuring in all the outer situations of our life? It is, on the other hand, the examination of the inner dynamics of our being. What is going on in our attitudes, our habits, our feelings, our emotions? What is taking place in our perceptions, our motives? In all these things, the inner (heart) and outer (lives), we open ourselves to God; we bring them before the Word; we let them sink down before the Word and be addressed by God. *M. Robert Mulholland, Shaped by the Word, pp. 119–27*

11

The Means of Grace

❖— *Scripture Sentence*
May grace and peace be yours in abundance.
1 Peter 1:2

❖— *Scripture Readings*

1 Peter 1:13-25
Hebrews 12:12-17
2 Corinthians 6:1-10
Acts 2:37-47

*2 Peter 1:3-11
Luke 22:14-23
Mark 6:45-52

❖— *Silence for Meditation*

❖— *Spiritual Reading*

❖— *Recording Insights and Commitments*

❖— *Prayers of Thanks, Intercession, Petition, and Praise*

❖— *Hymn Portion*
Come, let us use the grace divine, and all with one
accord, in perpetual covenant join ourselves to Christ
the Lord; give up ourselves, thru Jesus' power, his
name to glorify; and promise, in this sacred hour, for
God to live and die. *UMH #606*

❖— *Offering All of Life to God*

❖— *Closing Affirmation*
Forth in thy name, O Lord, I go, my daily labor to
pursue; thee, only thee, resolved to know in all I
think or speak or do. *Charles Wesley, UMH #438*

Reflections

The Christian life is impossible without God's grace extended to the believer. God is the seeker and always initiates every relationship with us. Even our awakening to God is a response to the Holy Spirit at work within us. God may choose to come to us, save us, provide for us, and hold us close to the divine in any way God chooses. We cannot control the ways or means that God will choose to use in our transformation any more than we can command God to transform us. However, we can choose to utilize those means of grace that have consistently been used by God to draw persons toward goodness and God. And unless we utilize these channels of sustenance, it is unlikely that we will experience the joy or fruit of discipleship.

Wesley believed that the grace of God was freely offered to all, and he believed that God used the means of grace to offer the fruits of grace to every believer. Therefore, no one had to suffer from unforgiven sin. No one had to walk alone. No one had to be a prisoner of fear. No one had to stay as she or he was. All could know sins forgiven. All could know the assurance and comfort of the Savior's presence in their lives. All could be redeemed and all could, by God's grace, travel the road to perfection. It was grace, God's grace, that made all of this possible.

God has chosen to use a variety of means to channel these gifts to us. It was Wesley's conviction that without regular use of the means of grace our relationship with God will be short-lived. Therefore, it is important for the Christian to use the means of grace with consistency. Wesley was convinced that an awakened heart will return to the old ways of rebellion and death without the regular practice of the means of grace. Humankind is not strong enough or good enough to go on to perfection without God's help. And God's help is available through the utilization of the means of grace.

Wesley identified means of grace in this way. "By means of grace I understand outward signs, words, or actions ordained of God and appointed for this end . . . to be the ordinary channels whereby he might convey to men preventing, justifying and sanctifying grace" *(Sermon 16, The Means of Grace Vol. 5, p. 197)*.

The means of grace give access to God's active presence in the world. They provide the pathway back to God for those who have wandered and prevent us from wandering away in the first place. The means of grace are given to us for our salvation, but they are gifts that we must use if we are to enjoy the benefit.

Wesley identified prayer, fasting, Bible study, hearing the preached word, and partaking of the Lord's Supper as essential means of grace for the hungry heart. While none of them is essential to our salvation, all can be used of God to enrich and transform our lives. To forsake them all is to find our spiritual life shriveled and lifeless.

If we were to ask Wesley why our relationship with God seems more distant than what the book of Acts describes, he would likely ask us if we are fully utilizing the means of grace. Do you want a more vital relationship with God? Use the means of grace. Do you long for the assurance of sins forgiven? Use the means of grace. Do you feel a great need for God's intervention in your life? Use the means of grace. Do you want to experience growth in your Christian life? Use the means of grace.

Following Christ was not easy in Wesley's time and it is not easy in our time. But God has made available for us the means of grace that permit us to stay connected with the One for whom all things are possible. It is inconceivable that we should live a transformed life without tapping into the resources of God to do that transforming work within us. Thomas Langford says that "grace is the specific expression of God's nature and will, an incarnate and continuing presence."

Need a little help in your Christian walk? Try using the means of grace daily for the next month. Read the Bible, pray personally and corporately, fast, worship, receive the sacrament, and I believe you will discover a multitude of resources entering your life through the disciplined use of the means of grace. While we cannot force God to love us, redeem us, or sustain us, we can, through the means of grace, place ourselves in a position to receive God's great and good gifts each day.

Spiritual Reading

Beware ... of imagining you shall obtain the end without using the means conducive to it. God can give the end without any means at all; but you have no reason to think he will. Therefore constantly and carefully use all those means which he has appointed to be the ordinary channels of his grace. Use every means which either reason or Scripture recommends, as conducive (through the free love of God in Christ) either to the obtaining or increasing any of the gifts of God. Thus expect a daily growth in that pure and holy religion which the world always did, and always will, call enthusiasm:—but which, to all who are saved from real enthusiasm, from merely nominal Christianity, is "the wisdom of God and the power of God;" a glorious image of the Most High; "righteousness and peace;" a "fountain of living water, springing up into everlasting life!" *Sermon 37, The Nature of Enthusiasm, Vol. 5, p. 478*

But of all the means of grace there is scarce any concerning which men have run into greater extremes, than that of which our Lord speaks in the above-mentioned words. I mean religious fasting. How have some exalted this beyond all Scripture and reason: — and others utterly disregarded it; as it were, revenging themselves by undervaluing as much as the former had overvalued it! Those have spoken of it, as if it were all in all; if not the end itself, yet infallibly connected with it: These, as if it were just nothing, as if it were a fruitless labour, which had no relation at all thereto. Whereas it is certain the truth lies between them both. It is not all, not yet is it nothing. It is not the end, but it is a precious means thereto; a means which God himself has ordained, and in which therefore, when it is duly used, he will surely give us his blessing. *Sermon 27, The Sermon on the Mount, Discourse 7, Vol. 5, p. 345*

Yet, as we find no command in holy writ for any particular order to be observed herein, so neither do the providence and the Spirit of God adhere to any without variation; but the means into which different men are led, and in which they find the blessing of God, are varied, transposed, and combined together, a thousand different ways. Yet still our wisdom is to follow the leadings of his providence and his Spirit; to be guided herein, (more especially as to the means wherein we ourselves seek the grace of God,) partly by his outward providence, giving us the opportunity of using sometimes one means, sometimes another, partly by our experience, which it is whereby his free Spirit is pleased most to work in our heart. And in the mean time, the sure and general rule for all who groan for the salvation of God is this, — whenever opportunity serves, use all the means which God has ordained; for who knows in which God will meet thee with the grace that bringeth salvation? *Sermon 16, The Means of Grace, Vol. 5, p. 200*

And that this is also an ordinary, stated means of receiving the grace of God, is evident from those words of the Apostle, which occur in the preceding chapter: "The cup of blessing which we bless, is it not the communion," or *communication*, "of the blood of Christ? The bread which we break, is it not the communion of the body of Christ?" (1 Cor. X. 16) Is not the eating of that bread, and the drinking of that cup, the outward, visible means, whereby God conveys into our souls all that spiritual grace, that righteousness, and peace, and joy in the Holy Ghost, which were purchased by the body of Christ once broken and the blood of Christ once shed for us? Let all, therefore, who truly desire the grace of God, eat of that bread, and drink of that cup. *Sermon 16, The Means of Grace, Vol. 5, p. 195*

But are there any ordinances now, since life and immortality were brought to light by the gospel? Are there, under the Christian dispensation, any means ordained of God, as the usual channels of his grace? This question could never have been proposed in the apostolical church, unless by one who openly avowed himself to be a Heathen; the whole body of Christians being agreed, that Christ had ordained certain outward means, for conveying his grace into the souls of men. Their constant practice set this beyond all dispute; for so long as "all that believed were together and had all things common," (Acts ii. 44,) "they continued steadfastly in the teaching of the Apostles, and in breaking of bread, and in prayers." (Verse 42) *Sermon 16, The Means of Grace, Vol. 5, p. 185*

He that hath the form of godliness, uses also the means of grace; yea, all of them, and at all opportunities. He constantly frequents the house of God; and that, not as the manner of some is, who come into the presence of the Most High, either loaded with gold and costly apparel, or in all the gaudy vanity of dress, and either by their unseasonable civilities to each other, or the impertinent gaiety of their behaviour, disclaim all pretensions to the form as well as to the power of godliness. Would to God there were none even among ourselves who fall under the same condemnation! Who come into this house, it may be, gazing about, or with all the signs of the most listless, careless indifference, though sometimes they may seem to use a prayer to God for his blessing on what they are entering upon; who, during that awful service, are either asleep, or reclined in the most convenient posture for it; or, as though they supposed God were asleep, talking with one another, or looking round, as utterly void of employment: Neither let these be accused of the form of godliness. No; he who has even this behaves with seriousness and attention in every part of that solemn service. More especially when he approaches the table of the Lord, it is not with a light or careless behaviour, but with an air, gesture, and deportment, which speaks nothing else but, "God be merciful to me, a sinner!" *Sermon 2, The Almost Christian, Vol. 5, p. 19*

Keep close, I beseech you, to every means of grace. Strive to walk in all the ordinances and commandments of God blameless, "giving all diligence to make your calling and election sure: Add to your faith virtue; to virtue knowledge; to knowledge temperance; to temperance patience; to patience godliness; to godliness brotherly kindness; to brotherly kindness charity." — For "if these things," says St. Peter, "be in you, and abound, they make you that you shall neither be barren nor unfruitful in the knowledge of our Lord Jesus Christ." Thus you will give the best token of your thankfulness to him for what he hath done for your souls; and you shall, not long hence, in heaven sing his praise with your happy brethren, gone thither before you. *Journal, Vol. 3, p. 88*

I showed, concerning the Holy Scriptures, 1. That to search, (that is, read and hear them,) is a command of God. 2. That this command is given to all, believers or unbelievers. 3. That this is commanded or ordained as a means of grace, a means of conveying the grace of God to all, whether unbelievers (such as those to whom he first gave this command, and those to whom faith cometh by hearing) or believers, who by experience know, that "all Scripture is profitable," or a means to this end, "that the man of God may be perfect, thoroughly furnished to all good works." *Journal, Vol. 1, p. 279*

In the afternoon I exhorted four or five thousand people at Bristol, neither to neglect nor rest in the means of grace. In the evening I endeavoured to lift up the hands that hung down, by declaring, "He will not break the bruised reed, nor quench the smoking flax." *Journal, Vol. 1, p. 249*

What is to be inferred from this undeniable matter of fact, —one that had not faith received it in the Lord's Supper? Why, 1. That there are means of grace, that is, outward ordinances, whereby the inward grace of God is ordinarily conveyed to man; whereby the faith that brings salvation is conveyed to them who before had it not. 2. That one of these means is the Lord's Supper. And, 3. That he who has not this faith ought to wait for it, in the use both of this, and of the other means which God hath ordained. *Journal, Vol. 1, p. 248*

The urge to find spiritual power and inner security without any major shift in lifestyle was as prevalent in the eighteenth century as it is today. Almost everyone would like to discover spiritual disciplines which would bring them answers to their problems, and a meaning in life without demanding that they give up a comfortable lifestyle....

Lifestyle questions are important because they remind us that the gifts of the Spirit are given not only to effect security and happiness, but primarily to enable the recipient of those gifts to share in God's work in this world. Spirit disciplines make clear that spiritual gifts are given for the blessings they bring to life. Indeed, these gifts when discovered within the community of the church confer onto each individual believer his or her unique identity.

Spiritual disciplines empty the self so the radiant spirit of God can enter in. Once the Spirit begins forming the person, works of sacrificial, caring love are the fruits. Wesley would have joined the Moravians if he could have accepted the spiritual blessings of God without the lifestyle of servanthood. He agreed with them that works were worthless to attain salvation, but insisted that they were the necessary results of the grace which made salvation possible. Gerald Craig suggests, "The Moravians had shown Wesley the true nature of saving faith. He was astonished that they seemed so blind to its necessary implications. Their Lutheran background made them recoil from anything suggestive of good works. Wesley believed that they were making the religious life a flight from responsibility."

If the desire for spiritual strength is not born out of concern for God's will, and a commitment to love and serve people, that strength will die. Spiritual strength increases to the extent God is in charge of a person's life and decreases in direct proportion if the person takes charge of his or her own life. Obedience becomes the key to both happiness and spiritual strength. Individuals become spiritually formed as their lives imitate the earthly ministry of Christ. *Blaine Taylor, John Wesley: A Blueprint for Church Renewal, pp. 12–14*

12
Holiness of Heart

❖— *Scripture Sentence*
Today, if you hear his voice, do not harden your hearts. *Hebrews 4:7*

❖— *Scripture Readings*

Deuteronomy 6:1-9	Acts 8:14-24
Mark 12:28-34	Ephesians 4:1-16
*Psalm 51:1-17	Philippians 2:1-11
Joel 2:12-13	

❖— *Silence for Meditation*

❖— *Spiritual Reading*

❖— *Recording of Insights and Commitments*

❖— *Prayers of Thanks, Intercession, Petition, and Praise*

❖— *Hymn Portion*
I want a principle within of watchful, godly fear, a sensibility of sin, a pain to feel it near. I want the first approach to feel of pride or wrong desire, to catch the wandering of my will, and quench the kindling fire. *UMH #410*

❖— *Offering All of Life to God*

❖— *Closing Affirmation*
Happy are those who do not follow the advice of the wicked, or take the path that sinners tread, or sit in the seat of scoffers; but their delight is in the law of the Lord, and on his law they meditate day and night. *Psalm 1:1-2*

——— *Reflections* ———

Holiness is an uncommon word in our vocabulary, but it was a central word and concept in the life and teaching of John Wesley. The seed was likely planted by his mother and was nurtured through a lifetime of study and seeking to be obedient to the will of God in every aspect of life.

To love God with all of one's being was clearly an idea that captured the attention of John Wesley early and stayed with him to the end. He believed and practiced that loving God with all of the heart was the foundation for all other Christian living. Again and again he returned to this theme. When speaking of sanctification or Christian perfection, he was working on the foundation of holiness of heart and life that he believed was the very epitome of Christian living.

Holiness is not only an uncommon word but a word that triggers unpleasant images of persons who claimed the concept but whose lives were anything but holy. We can tolerate almost anything more easily than a "holier than thou" attitude. But the holiness of heart about which Wesley speaks and which he pursued for all of his life is something quite different. Holiness of heart was marked by purity and unparalleled devotion to God in Christ, and it resulted in the holiness of all of life.

Inward and outward holiness are inseparable because all actions and attitudes find their root in the heart. Thus a holy, pure, committed heart will lead to a life that reflects this holiness in all aspects and activities of the daily journey. Holiness of heart is a prerequisite that leads unquestionably to holiness of life.

It is not unusual to dismiss the concept of holiness of heart as being too otherworldly or too far removed from the activistic life style that most of us live. And yet when we follow such a course we discover that without a heart given to God, even our efforts at reflecting God's light are often hopelessly inadequate. Only when God in Christ is embraced as only Savior, only Lord, and only necessary companion in all of life, only then can our outward actions be trusted to reflect God's light.

Faithfulness to God was a lifelong quest for the Wesley brothers. They learned from study and experience that this journey of faithfulness begins in the heart. When the heart is holy, all of life is transformed. God is holy and we depend upon God's grace to travel the road toward a holy heart.

Holiness of heart opens us to the direction of the Holy Spirit, gives the assurance of sins forgiven and life held close and secure in the hands of God. Holiness of heart is the beginning, but as we shall see, there is much more to come.

——— *Spiritual Reading* ———

When I was about twenty-two, my father pressed me to enter into holy orders. At the same time, the providence of God directing me to Kempis's "Christian Pattern," I began to see, that true religion was seated in the heart, and that God's law extended to all our thoughts as well as words and actions. I was, however, very angry at Kempis, for being too strict; though I read him only in Dean Stanhope's translation. Yet I had frequently much sensible comfort in reading him, such as I was an utter stranger to before: And meeting likewise with a religious friend, which I never had till now, I began to alter the whole form of my conversation, and to set in earnest upon a new life. I set apart an hour or two a day for religious retirement. I communicated every week. I watched against all sin, whether in word or deed. I began to aim at, and pray for, inward holiness. So that now, "doing so much, and living so good a life," I doubted not but I was a good Christian. *Journal, Vol. 1, p. 99*

Not that this forbids us to love anything besides God: It implies that we love our brother also. Nor yet does it forbid us (as some have strangely imagined) to take pleasure in any thing but God. To suppose this, is to suppose the Fountain of holiness is directly the author of sin; since he has inseparably annexed pleasure to the use of those creatures which are necessary to sustain the life he has given us. This, therefore, can never be the meaning of his command. What the real sense of it is, both our blessed Lord and his Apostles tell us too frequently, and too plainly, to be misunderstood. They all with one mouth bear witness, that the true meaning of those several declarations, "The Lord thy God is one Lord:" "Thou shalt have no other gods but me:" "Thou shalt love the Lord thy God with all thy strength:" "Thou shalt cleave unto him:" "The desire of thy soul shall be to his name:"—is no other than this: The one perfect Good shall be your ultimate end. One thing shall ye desire for its own sake, — the fruition of Him that is All in all. One happiness shall ye propose to your souls, even an union with Him that made them: the having "fellowship with the Father and the Son:" the being joined to the Lord in one Spirit. One design you are to pursue to the end of time,— the enjoyment of God in time and eternity. Desire other things, so far as they tend to this. *Sermon 17, Circumcision of the Heart, Vol. 5, p. 207*

But the most common of all the enthusiasts of this kind, are those who imagine themselves Christians, and are not. These abound, not only in all parts of our land, but in most parts of the habitable earth. That they are not Christians is clear and undeniable, if we believe the oracles of God. For Christians are holy; these are unholy; Christians love God; these love the world: Christians are humble, these are proud; Christians are gentle; these are passionate; Christians have the mind which was in Christ; these are at the utmost distance from it. Consequently, they are no more Christians, than they are archangels. Yet they imagine themselves so to be; and they can give several reasons for it: For they have been *called* so ever since they can remember; they were christened many years ago; they embrace the *Christian opinions*, vulgarly termed the Christian or Catholic faith; they use the *Christian modes of worship*, as their fathers did before them; they live what is called, a good *Christian life*, as the rest of their neighbours do. And who shall presume to think or say that these men are not Christians? — though without one grain of true faith in Christ, or of real, inward holiness; without ever having tasted the love of God, or been "made partakers of the Holy Ghost!" *Sermon 37, The Nature of Enthusiasm, Vol. 5, p. 471*

From Gal. vi. 3, I earnestly warned all who had tasted the grace of God, 1. Not to think they were justified, before they had a clear assurance that God had forgiven their sins; bringing in a calm peace, the love of God, and dominion over all sin. 2. Not to think themselves any thing after they had this; but to press forward for the prize of their high calling, even a clean heart, thoroughly renewed after the image of God, in righteousness and true holiness. *Journal, Vol. 1., p. 284*

In 1727 I read Mr. Law's "Christian Perfection," and "Serious Call," and more explicitly resolved to be all devoted to God, in body, soul, and spirit. In 1730 I began to be homo unius libri; (1) to study (comparatively) no book but the Bible. I then saw, in a stronger light than ever before, that only one thing is needful, even faith that worketh by the love of God and man, all inward and outward holiness; and I groaned to love God with all my heart, and to serve Him with all my strength. *Journal, Vol. 3, p. 213*

Yet, on the authority of God's word, and our own Church, I must repeat the question, "Hast thou received the Holy Ghost?" If thou hast not, thou art not yet a Christian. For a Christian is a man that is "anointed with the Holy Ghost and with power." Thou art not yet made a partaker of pure religion and undefiled. Dost thou know what religion is? that it is a participation of the divine nature; the life of God in the soul of man; Christ formed in the heart: "Christ in thee, the hope of glory?" happiness and holiness; heaven begun on earth? "a kingdom of God within thee; not meat and drink," no outward thing; "but righteousness, and peace, and joy in the Holy Ghost?" an everlasting kingdom brought into thy soul. *Sermon 3, Awake, Thou that Sleepest, Vol. 5, p. 30*

Now, "this word is nigh thee." This condition of life is plain, easy, always at hand. "It is in thy mouth, and in thy heart," through the operation of the Spirit of God. The moment "thou believest in thine heart" in him whom God "hath raised from the dead," and "confessest with thy mouth the Lord Jesus" as *thy* Lord and *thy* God, "thou shalt be saved" from condemnation, from the guilt and punishment of thy former sins, and shalt have power to serve God in true holiness all the remaining days of thy life. *Sermon 6, The Righteousness of Faith, Vol. 5, p. 69*

But suppose perfect obedience, for the time to come, could atone for the sins that are past, this would profit thee nothing; for thou art not able to perform it; no, not in any one point. Begin now: Make the trial. Shake off that outward sin that so easily besetteth thee. Thou canst not. How then wilt thou change thy life from all evil to all good? Indeed, it is impossible to be done, unless first thy heart be changed. For, so long as the tree remains evil, it cannot bring forth good fruit. But art thou able to change thy own heart, from all sin to all holiness? To quicken a soul that is dead in sin, — dead to God, and alive only to the world? No more than thou art able to quicken thy soul in any degree, no more than to give any degree of life to the dead body. Thou canst do nothing, more or less, in this matter; thou art utterly without strength. To be deeply sensible of this, how helpless thou art, as well as how guilty and how sinful—this is that "repentance not to be repented of," which is the forerunner of the kingdom of God. *Sermon 7, The Way to the Kingdom, Vol. 5, p. 84*

That the testimony of the Spirit of God must, in the very nature of things, be antecedent to the testimony of our own spirit, may appear from this single consideration: We must be holy in heart and life before we can be conscious that we are so. But we must love God before we can be holy at all, this being the root of all holiness. Now we cannot love God, till we know he loves us: "We love him, because he first loved us:" And we cannot know his love to us, till his Spirit witnesses it to our spirit. Till then we cannot believe it; we cannot say, "The life which I now live, I live by faith in the son of God, who loved me, and gave himself for me." *Sermon 11, The Witness of the Spirit, Vol. 5, p. 127*

St. Peter expresses it in a still different manner, though to the same effect: "As he that hath called you is holy, so be ye holy in all manner of conversation." (1 Peter 1.15.) According to this Apostle, then, perfection is another name for universal holiness: Inward and outward righteousness: Holiness of life, arising from holiness of heart. *Sermon 76, On Perfection, Vol. 6, p. 414*

Whereas in that moment when we are justified freely by his grace, when we are accepted through the Beloved, we are born again, born from above, born of the Spirit. And there is as great a change wrought in our souls when we are born of the Spirit, as was wrought in our bodies when we are born of a woman. There is, in that hour, a general change from inward sinfulness, to inward holiness. The love of the creature is changed to the love of the Creator; the love of the world into the love of God. Earthly desires, the desire of the flesh, the desire of the eyes, and the pride of life, are, in that instant, changed, by the mighty power of God, into heavenly desires. The whirlwind of our will is stopped in its mid career, and sinks down into the will of God. Pride and haughtiness subside into lowliness of heart; as do anger, with all turbulent and unruly passions, into calmness, meekness, and gentleness. In a word, the earthly, sensual, devilish mind, gives place to "the mind that was in Christ Jesus." *Sermon 83, On Patience, Vol. 6, p. 488*

It is, then, a great blessing given to this people, that as they do not think or speak of justification so as to supersede sanctification, so neither do they think or speak of sanctification so as to supersede justification. They take care to keep each in its own place, laying equal stress on one and the other. They know God has joined these together, and it is not for man to put them asunder: Therefore they maintain, with equal zeal and diligence, the doctrine of free, full, present justification, on the one hand, and of entire sanctification both of heart and life, on the other; being as tenacious of inward holiness as any Mystic, and of outward, as any Pharisee. *Sermon 107, On God's Vineyard, Vol. 7, p. 205*

Wesley's evangelistic preaching, like his pastoral care, related to the individual although it was frequently delivered before large congregations of listeners. Wesley's preaching was meant as direct discourse to the individual person and as a call to conversion. Analogously, Wesley's social work and ethical preaching focused first on the individual, then the entire English nation, other nations, and finally human society, regardless of its structure, culture, or political and economic order. They were social in the sense of eliminating social distresses and referring to life with other persons and in society. Nevertheless, the temporal and substantive priority doubtless lay with individual renewal, which preceded social renewal as its necessary precondition. Admittedly, individual renewal acquired its meaning through more than just the social effects it produced. Nevertheless, according to Wesley's pointedly formulated statement about Christianity as "essentially a social religion," no real transformation of an individual by God's grace could fail to immediately affect the shared life of all people. The aim of Wesley's preaching was therefore twofold: to lead individuals to renewal through God's grace in justification and sanctification and thus to a meaningful life, and to guide them into activity suited to transform the whole of society from within. *Manfred Marquardt, John Wesley's Social Ethics, p. 119*

13

Preventing Grace

❖— *Scripture Sentence*
 I will pour out my Spirit upon all flesh. *Acts 2:17*

❖— *Scripture Readings*

*Acts 16:6-10	Acts 8:26-40
John 16:1-15	Acts 17:16-31
1 Samuel 3:2-18	Luke 24:13-35
Mark 4:1-9	

❖— *Silence for Meditation*

❖— *Spiritual Reading*

❖— *Recording of Insights and Commitments*

❖— *Prayers of Thanks, Intercession, Petition, and Praise*

❖— *Hymn Portion*
 There for me the Savior stands, shows his wounds
 and spreads his hands. God is love! I know, I feel;
 Jesus weeps and loves me still. *UMH #355*

❖— *Offering All of Life to God*

❖— *Closing Affirmation*
 Lord, you have been our dwelling place in all generations. *Psalm 90:1*

——— *Reflections* ———

No one is ever outside the reach of God's loving presence. Even though we may try to place ourselves beyond the gaze of God, the psalmist reminds us it is impossible. "If I ascend to heaven, you are there; if I make my bed in Sheol, you are there. If I take the wings of the morning and settle at the farthest limits of the sea, even there your hand shall lead me, and your right hand shall hold me fast" (Psalm 139:8-10).

Not only is it impossible to step outside God's gracious reach but God is always actively engaged on our behalf. God's right hand does hold us fast, no matter how far we stray from God's grand design for us, a design that was in place even before the foundation of the world (Eph. 1:4-5).

It was the conviction of God's preventing grace (often referred to as prevenient grace today) that led John Wesley to believe that everyone had within them this mark of divinity that could not be extinguished. He believed that God is active on our behalf and in our lives whether we recognize it or not.

Our lives are shaped by the God we worship. If we give allegiance to an absent, cool, distant, and uncaring God, we may feel cut off, alone, unprotected, and uncared for. On the other hand, if we worship a God who loves us without condition, walks with us even when we deny Divine Presence, who is actively engaged for the good of all humankind (even me), we will find an assurance, peace, and joy in every condition of life that we experience.

Most mature Christians look back at their lives and see that God has indeed prevented them from painful mistakes, kept them from unworthy goals, and guided them and the events around them, even though they were unaware of God's nearness and intervention on their behalf. They also testify that *God* apprehended *them,* rather than the other way around. It was God who sought them out, wooed their attention, and called forth their love.

It is this awakening call, this divine spark within, this active involvement in all of life that today is called prevenient grace. And it is this unmerited action of God within and without that makes it possible for us to respond to God, know God, and walk in companionship with God. Each one of us is this very moment experiencing the active involvement of God within our lives and on our behalf in the world in which we live. Were God to withhold this grace, we would no longer *be*. It is this grace of God that calls forth our own response of love, faith and desire to walk with God in Christ. Today, in more ways than we will ever know, God is seeking our response. What shall we do? John Wesley and countless Christians before and after him would say, "Repent, believe, and offer your life to God in Christ anew this very moment." This is the appropriate and faithful response to God's prevenient grace.

At what time I became a subject to my own will, I cannot ascertain; but from that time in many things I offended. First, against my parents; next, against God! And that I was preserved from outward evils, was not owing to the purity of my own will; but the grace of Christ preventing and overruling me. *Journal, Vol. 3, p. 140*

If we take this in its utmost extent, it will include all that is wrought in the soul by what is frequently termed natural conscience, but more properly, preventing grace:—all the drawings of the Father; the desires after God, which, if we yield to them, increase more and more:—all that light wherewith the Son of God "enlighteneth every one that cometh into the world:" showing every man "to do justly, to love mercy, and to walk humbly with his God:"—all the convictions which his Spirit, from time to time, works in every child of man; although, it is true, the generality of men stifle them as soon as possible, and after a while forget, or at least deny, that they ever had them at all. *Sermon 43, The Scripture Way of Salvation, Vol. 6, p. 44*

One thing more is implied in this repentance; namely, a conviction of our helplessness, of our utter inability to think one good thought, or to form one good desire; and much more to speak one word aright, or to perform one good action, but through his free almighty grace, first preventing us, and then accompanying us every moment. *Sermon 43, The Scripture Way of Salvation, Vol. 6, p. 51*

For allowing that all the souls of men are dead in sin by nature, this excuses none, seeing there is no man that is in a state of mere nature; there is no man, unless he has quenched the Spirit, that is wholly void of the grace of God. No man living is entirely destitute of what is vulgarly called *natural conscience*. But this is not natural: It is more properly termed, *preventing grace*. Every man has a greater or less measure of this, which waiteth not for the call of man. Every one has, sooner or later, good desires; although the generality of men stifle them before they can strike deep root, or produce any considerable fruit. Every one has some measure of that light, some faint glimmering ray, which, sooner or later, more or less, enlightens every man that cometh into the world. And every one, unless he be one of the small number whose conscience is seared as with a hot iron, feels more or less uneasy when he acts contrary to the light of his own conscience. So that no man sins because he has not grace, but because he does not use the grace which he hath. *Sermon 85, On Working out Our own Salvation, Vol. 6, p. 512*

The First I shall mention, as being more especially grievous to the Holy Spirit, is inconsiderateness and inadvertence to his holy motions within us. There is a particular frame and temper of soul, a sobriety of mind, with which the Spirit of God will not concur in the purifying of our hearts. It is in our power, through his preventing and assisting grace, to prepare this in ourselves; and he expects we should, this being the foundation of all his after-works. Now, this consists in preserving our minds in a cool and serious disposition, in regulating and calming our affections, and calling in and checking the inordinate pursuits of our passions after the vanities and pleasures of this world; the doing of which is of such importance, that the very reason why men profit so little under the most powerful means, is, that they do not look enough within themselves,—they do not observe and watch the discords and imperfections of their own spirits, nor attend with care to the directions and remedies which the Holy Spirit is always ready to suggest. Men are generally lost in the hurry of life, in the business or pleasures of it, and seem to think that their regeneration, their new nature, will spring and grow up within them, with as little care and thought of their own as their bodies were conceived and have attained their full strength and stature; whereas, there is nothing more certain than that the Holy Spirit will not purify our nature, unless we carefully attend to his motions, which are lost upon us while, in the Prophet's language, we "scatter away our time,"—while we squander away our thoughts upon unnecessary things, and leave our spiritual improvement, the one thing needful, quite unthought of and neglected. *Sermon 138, On Grieving the Holy Spirit, Vol. 7, p. 489*

Wherefore we have no power to do good works, pleasant and acceptable to God, without the grace of God by Christ preventing us, that we may have a good-will, and working with us when we have that good will. *A Farther Appeal to Men of Reason and Religion, Vol. 8, p. 53*

Men may have many good tempers, and a blameless life, (speaking in a loose sense,) by nature and habit, with preventing grace; and yet not have faith and the love of God. *Some Late Conversations, IV, Vol. 8, p. 293*

For the preventing grace of God, which is common to all, is sufficient to bring us to Christ, though it is not sufficient to carry us any further till we are justified. *The Principles of a Methodist, Vol. 8, p. 373*

I showed at large, (1.) That the Lord's supper was ordained by God to be a means of conveying to men either preventing, or justifying, or sanctifying grace, according to their several necessities. (2.) That the persons for whom it was ordained, are all those who know and feel that they want the grace of God, either to restrain them from sin, or to show their sins forgiven, or to renew their souls in the image of God. (3.) That, inasmuch as we come to his table, not to give him anything, but to receive whatsoever he sees best for us, there is no previous preparation indispensably necessary, but a desire to receive whatsoever he pleases to give. And, (4.) That no fitness is required at the time of communicating, but a sense of our state, of our utter sinfulness and helplessness. *Journal, Vol. 1, p. 280*

One of Mr. Fletcher's Checks considers at large the Calvinistic supposition, "that a natural man is as dead as a stone;" and shows the utter falseness and absurdity of it; seeing no man living is without some preventing grace; and every degree of grace is a degree of life. *Letter to Mr. John Mason, Vol. 12, p. 453*

All this may easily be accounted for. At first, curiosity brings many hearers; at the same time, God draws many by his preventing grace to hear his word, and comforts them in hearing. One then tells another. By this means, on the one hand, curiosity spreads and increases; and, on the other, the drawings of God's Spirit touch more hearts, and many of them more powerfully than before. He now offers grace to all that hear, most of whom are in some measure affected, and, more or less moved with approbation of what they hear, have a desire to please God, with good-will to his messenger. And these principles, variously combined and increasing, raise the general work to its highest point. *A Short History of the People Called Methodists, Vol. 13, p. 338*

The general manner wherein it pleases God to set it up in the heart is this: A sinner, being drawn by the love of the Father, enlightened by the Son, ("the true light which lighteth every man that cometh into the world,") and convinced of sin by the Holy Ghost; through the preventing grace which is given him freely, cometh weary and heavy laden, and casteth all his sins upon Him that is "mighty to save." He receiveth from Him true, living faith. Being justified by faith, he hath peace with God: He rejoices in hope of the glory of God, and knows that sin hath no more dominion over him. And the love of God is shed abroad in his heart, producing all holiness of heart and of conversation. *Works Abridged From Various Authors by John Wesley, Vol. 14, p. 212*

For Wesley, prevenient grace was most fundamentally revealed in moral conscience: But what does this imply for moral action or faithful response? There has been diversity of interpretation. On one end of a spectrum, one can find an understanding of prevenient grace as a power given to human beings, an endowment of ability to take initiative and act righteously. There is no longer a "natural man," but only a graciously capable person. The emphasis in this case is on the power of humans to initiate movement toward God. In the middle position, prevenient grace is intepreted as a conscience that can evoke repentance; people are, by grace, aware of their fallen condition and may or may not respond to God's gracious overture. Response, rather than initiative, is emphasized. At the other end of the spectrum, prevenient grace has been interpreted in a more restrictive manner. Faith is altogether a gracious gift of God. The freedom of sinful humanity is only the liberty of rebellion; it is wholly negative. This freedom leads to despair; human inability is recognized, thanks to prevenient grace; and also, thanks to prevenient grace, humans cease to resist, and God's causality is able to operate. *Thomas A. Langford, Practical Divinity, p. 33*

Prevenient grace is an effect of the atonement of Jesus Christ. The grace of God in Christ creates a new possibility for human life, and to every human life God is antecedently and enablingly present. Charles Wesley expressed this:

> Long my imprisoned spirit lay,
> Fast bound in sin and nature's night;
> Thine eye diffused a quickening ray,
> I woke, the dungeon flamed with light:
> My chains fell off, my heart was free,
> I rose, went forth, and followed thee.

... There was for Wesley an "order of salvation," a dynamic movement of the Christian life from its inception to its fulfillment. Moving from conscience to conviction of sin, to repentance, to justification, to regeneration, to sanctification, to glorification, there is a pattern of gracious development. This development is built upon the active presence of the Holy Spirit as it encounters, wins assent, and transforms life. Hence justification results in regeneration. Forgiveness brings a changed condition of life. The old nature is set aside as new creation occurs. Those who are redeemed have been given a new nature, for they have had restored in them the image of God. Wesley was emphatic about the change that God's grace effects in human life; it is characteristic of his thought that he placed great emphasis upon the new life in Christ. This altered status is the most important fact of human existence; grace has changed the affections, the mind, and the will. Christians are new creatures, set once more in proper relationship with God and their neighbors. *Thomas A. Langford, Practical Divinity, pp. 34–36*

14

Forgiveness

❖— *Scripture Sentence*
Then he opened their minds to understand the scriptures, and he said to them, "Thus it is written, that the Messiah is to suffer and to rise from the dead on the third day, and that repentance and forgiveness of sins is to be proclaimed in his name to all nations." *Luke 24:45-47*

❖— *Scripture Readings*

Matthew 6:7-14	Acts 10:34-43
*1 John 1:5-10	Luke 5:1-26
Psalm 103:1-14	Mark 11:20-26
Colossians 2:8-15	

❖— *Silence for Meditation*

❖— *Spiritual Reading*

❖— *Recording Insights and Commitments*

❖— *Prayers of Thanks, Intercession, Petition, and Praise*

❖— *Hymn Portion*
Plenteous grace with thee is found, grace to cover all my sin; let the healing streams abound, make and keep me pure within. Thou of life the fountain art, freely let me take of thee; spring thou up within my heart; rise to all eternity. *UMH #479*

❖— *Offering All of Life to God*

❖— *Closing Affirmation*
I am writing to you little children because your sins are forgiven on account of his name. *1 John 2:12*

——— *Reflections* ———

We don't spend much time talking about sin in our culture. We should, however, for sin is real, contagious, and deadly. Unforgiven sin is a burden too heavy for any of us to carry. It leaves little room for joy and assurance in the life of a Christian. Unforgiven sin often lingers in the shadows of our lives, constantly reminding us of our inadequacy, our incompleteness, and our unworthiness. The longer we put off dealing with sin and forgiveness, the more difficult it is for us to receive this free gift of grace.

Many of us carry the mistaken notion that forgiveness is something we earn or is available only to people already perfect. We hear the words of forgiveness at the Lord's Table but find it hard to believe that our sin can be or is forgiven. There are even those who stay away from the table because they feel their sin is too great to be forgiven. Still others make light of sin, considering our turning away from God a natural consequence of living in the modern world. By turning away from God, refusing to look to God or to admit that God exists and looks at us, some think they can blot out the reality and the consequences of sin.

And yet each of us is made for communion with God; it is deep in our nature to desire God and to walk with God. We are, indeed, as Saint Augustine said, restless until we find rest in God. And the emptiness that many feel can only be filled or satisfied by God. Whenever we turn away from God we turn away from order, goodness, and life and turn toward chaos, evil, and death. Thus, without God in the center of life, we become easy prey to the sins of mind, heart, and body.

The Wesley brothers had no doubt about the reality of sin, but it took them some time to discover the reality of forgiveness. We should not be surprised that our experience is similar to theirs. The faith and confidence in God's ability and desire to forgive any sin was slow in coming; but gradually the light dawned. It is true, we are justified by grace through faith. Our hope for forgiveness does not depend on our merit but on Jesus Christ's merit. Forgiveness and salvation, as life itself, are pure gifts. Nothing we can do will earn our salvation or our forgiveness.

In a culture that applauds independence, self-reliance, and self-centeredness, it is difficult to admit that we are hopeless and helpless without the saving work of Christ within us. We often carry burdens of unresolved guilt and unforgiven sin, wondering why we miss the joy, assurance, confidence, and strength in God that others witness to.

The good news dawned on the Wesley brothers in the month of May 1738. Following his Aldersgate experience, John reports the change in his life this way:

> In the evening I went very unwillingly to a society in Aldersgate Street where one was reading Luther's preface to the Epistle to the Romans. About a quarter before nine, while he was describing the change which God works in the heart through faith in Christ, I felt my heart strangely warmed. I felt I did trust in Christ, Christ alone for salvation: And an assurance was given me, that he had taken away my sins, even mine, and saved me from the law of sin and death (*Journal, Vol. 1, p. 103*).

Carrying the baggage of unforgiven sin or the weight of our refusal to forgive others is a burden that can squeeze joy out of our lives. But the good news we proclaim is that the assurance of sins forgiven is a gift God is eager to give to us all. It is a message that we need to hear often and will as we listen to the Wesleys' witness.

——— *Spiritual Reading* ———

I showed at large, in order to answer those who taught that none but they who are full of faith and the Holy Ghost ought ever to communicate, (1.) That the Lord's Supper was ordained by God to be a means of conveying to men either preventing, or justifying, or sanctifying grace, according to their several necessities. (2.) That the persons for whom it was ordained are all those who know and feel that they want the grace of God, either to restrain them from sin, or to "show their sins forgiven," or to "renew their souls" in the image of God. (3.) That inasmuch as we come to his table, not to give him anything, but to receive whatsoever he sees best for us, there is no previous preparation indispensably necessary, but a desire to receive whatsoever he pleases to give. *A Letter to the Lord Bishop of London, Vol. 8, p. 486*

Here I found the peace I had long sought in vain; for I was assured my sins were forgiven. Not indeed all at once, but by degrees; not in one moment, nor in one hour. For I could not immediately believe that I was forgiven, because of the mistake I was then in concerning forgiveness. I saw not then, that the first promise to the children of God is, "Sin shall no more reign over you;" but thought I was to feel it in me no more from the time it was forgiven. Therefore, although I had the mastery over it, yet I often feared it was not forgiven, because it still stirred in me, and at some times thrust sore at me that I might fall: Because, though it did not reign, it did remain in me; and I was continually tempted, though not overcome. *Journal, Vol. 1, p. 121*

I talked largely with my mother, who told me, that, till a short time since, she had scarce heard such a thing mentioned, as the having forgiveness of sins now, or God's Spirit bearing witness with our spirit: Much less did she imagine that this was the common privilege of all true believers. "Therefore," said she, "I never durst ask it for myself. But two or three weeks ago, while my son Hall was pronouncing those words, in delivering the cup to me. 'The blood of our Lord Jesus Christ, which was given for thee:' the words struck through my heart, and I knew God for

Christ's sake had forgiven me all my sins." *Journal, Vol. 1, p. 223*

And now first it was that I had that full assurance of my own reconciliation to God, through Christ. For many years I had had the forgiveness of my sins, and a measure of the grace of God; but I had not till now that witness of his Spirit, which shuts out all doubt and fear. In all my trials I had always a confidence in Christ, who had done so great things for me. But it was a confidence mixed with fear: I was afraid I had not done enough. There was always something dark in my soul till now. But now the clear light shined; and I saw that what I had hitherto so constantly insisted on,—the *doing* so much and *feeling* so much, the long repentance and preparation for believing, the bitter sorrow for sin, and that deep contrition of heart which is found in some,—were by no means essential to justification. Yea, that wherever the free grace of God is rightly preached, a sinner in the full career of his sins will probably receive it, and be justified by it, before one who insists on such previous preparation. *Journal, Vol. 1, p. 128*

About three in the afternoon, I came to Mr. Benjamin Seward's, at Bengeworth, near Evesham. At five, I expounded in his house (part of the thirteenth chapter of the first of Corinthians,) and at seven, in the school-house; where I invited all who "had nothing to pay," to come and accept of free forgiveness. In the morning I preached near Mr. Seward's house, to a small serious congregation, on those words, "I came not to call the righteous, but sinners to repentance." *Journal, Vol. 1, p. 228*

But this is the Third thing which was to be considered, namely, Who are they that are justified? And the Apostle tells us expressly, the ungodly: "He (that is, God) justifieth the ungodly;" the ungodly of every kind and degree; and none but the ungodly. As "they that are righteous need no repentance," so they need no forgiveness. It is only sinners that have any occasion for pardon: It is sin alone which admits of being forgiven. Forgiveness, therefore, has an immediate reference to sin, and, in this respect, to nothing else. It is our *unrighteousness* to which the pardoning God is *merciful*: It is our *iniquity* which he "remembereth no more." *Sermon 5, Justification by Faith, Vol. 5, p. 58*

Above all, how long wilt thou forget, that whatsoever thou doest, or whatsoever thou hast, before thy sins are forgiven thee, it avails nothing with God toward the procuring of thy forgiveness? Yea, and that it must all be cast behind thy back, trampled under foot, made no account of, or thou wilt never find favour in God's sight; because, until then, thou canst not ask it, as a mere sinner, guilty, lost, undone, having nothing to plead, nothing to offer to God, but only the merits of his well-beloved Son, "who loved *thee,* and gave himself for *thee!*" *Sermon 6, The Righteousness of Faith, Vol. 5, p. 76*

"As we forgive them that trespass against us."—In these words our Lord clearly declares both on what condition, and in what degree or manner, we may look to be forgiven of God. All our trespasses and sins are forgiven us, *if* we forgive, and as we forgive, others. This is a point of the utmost importance. And our blessed Lord is so jealous lest at any time we should let it slip out of our thoughts, that he not only inserts it in the body of his prayer, but presently after repeats it twice over. "If," saith he, "ye forgive men their trespasses, your heavenly Father will also forgive you: But if ye forgive not men their trespasses, neither will your Father forgive your trespasses." (Verses 14, 15.) Secondly, God forgives us *as* we forgive others. So that if any malice or bitterness, if any taint of unkindness or anger remains, if we do not clearly, fully, and from the heart, forgive all men their trespasses, we so far cut short the forgiveness of our own: God cannot clearly and fully forgive us: He may show us some degree of mercy; but we will not suffer him to blot out all our sins, and forgive all our iniquities. *Sermon 26, Sermon on the Mount, Discourse 6, Vol. 5, p. 340*

The grace of God given herein confirms to us the pardon of our sins, and enables us to leave them. As our bodies are strengthened by bread and wine, so are our souls by these tokens of the body and the blood of Christ. This is the food of our souls: This gives strength to perform our duty, and leads us on to perfection. If, therefore, we have any regard for the plain command of Christ, if we desire the pardon of our sins, if we wish for strength to believe, to love and obey God, then we should neglect no opportunity of receiving the Lord's Supper; then we must never turn our backs on the feast which our Lord has prepared for us. We must neglect no occasion, which the good providence of God affords us, for this purpose. This is the true rule: So often are we to receive as God gives us opportunity. Whoever, therefore, does not receive, but goes from the holy table, when all things are prepared, either does not understand his duty, or does not care for the divine command of his Saviour, the forgiveness of his sins, the strengthening of his soul, and the refreshing it with the hope of glory. *Sermon 101, The Duty of Constant Communion, Vol. 7, p. 148*

A confidence then in a pardoning God is essential to saving faith. The forgiveness of sins is one of the first of those unseen things whereof faith is the evidence. And if you are sensible of this, will you quarrel with us concerning an indifferent circumstance of it? Will you think it an important objection, that we assert that this faith is usually given in a moment? First, let me entreat you to read over that authentic account of God's dealings with men, the Acts of the Apostles. In this treatise you will find how he wrought from the beginning on those who received remission of sins by faith. *An Earnest Appeal to Men of Reason and Religion, Vol. 8, p. 24*

Indeed, the leading of the Spirit is different in different souls. His more usual method, I believe, is, to give, in one and the same moment, forgiveness of sins, and a full assurance of that forgiveness. Yet in many he works as he did in me; giving first the remission of sins, and after some weeks, or months, or years, the full assurance of it. *The Principles of a Methodist, Vol. 8, p. 371*

We implore thy tender mercies in the forgiveness of all our sins, whereby we have offended either in thought, word, or deed. We desire to be truly sorry for all our misdoings, and

utterly to renounce whatsoever is contrary to thy will. We desire to devote our whole man, body, soul, and spirit, to thee. And as thou dost inspire us with these desires, so accompany them always with thy grace, that we may every day, with our whole hearts, give ourselves up to thy service.
A Collection of Prayers for Families, Vol. 11, p. 241

15

Holiness of Life

❖— *Scripture Sentence*
As he who called you is holy, be holy yourselves in all your conduct. *1 Peter 1:15*

❖— *Scripture Readings*

1 Thessalonians 4:1-12	Romans 12:1-8
James 1:19-27	*Romans 12:9-21
2 Peter 1:3-11	Matthew 25:31-46
Hebrews 12:1-16	

❖— *Silence for Meditation*

❖— *Spiritual Reading*

❖— *Recording Insights and Commitments*

❖— *Prayers of Thanks, Intercession, Petition, and Praise*

❖— *Hymn Portion*
Let us for each other care, each the other's burdens bear; to thy church the pattern give, show how true believers live. *UMH #562*

❖— *Offering All of Life to God*

❖— *Closing Affirmation*
Religion that is pure and undefiled before God, the Father, is this: to care for orphans and widows in their distress, and to keep oneself unstained by the world. *James 1:27*

—— Reflections ——

Many assert that John Wesley was the world's most influential social reformer of his day. While some will question the depth of his influence, none question his remarkable ability to link piety with justice and to translate doctrine into daily living. From the early days at Oxford until a few days before his death, Wesley was about the ministry of caring for the poor, the oppressed, and the imprisoned. And all of this while living a rigorous life of prayer, study, and reflection.

This commitment to neighbor and passion to proclaim the gospel story was so great that John and Charles rode in a cart with a condemned prisoner so that they could sing and pray on the way to the hangman's scaffold (Heitzenrater, *Wesley and the People Called Methodists*, p. 124).

Holy living is a direct result of and inseparable from a holy heart. To experience Christian perfection is to live as Jesus lived. It is to be obedient to the One proclaimed as Savior and Lord. Matthew 25 is a text to be taken seriously. To know Christ and to be known by Christ means to walk with Christ in the everyday business of life.

Certainly one of the goals of the societies, bands, and classes was to help people live the holy life. While each had some distinctive characteristics there was one common purpose. The meetings, the confessions, the prayers, the admonishment, the encouragement, the teaching were all designed to aid the participant in the translation of the gospel story into everyday living. To fail to practice holy living was to place in jeopardy one's relationship to God.

As early as the Oxford Holy Club days the spiritual quest for holiness centered in a pure heart and a transformed life. This transformed life within led to a transformed life without. For the Wesleys the only reasonable response to God's grace and activity within was a faithful living out, an imitation of the One "who went about doing good." Obedience to Christ meant seeking to fashion all of life in keeping with the life of Jesus. Such obedience translated naturally into a life of holiness where love of God and love of neighbor were the guiding principle and the evident fruit of faith in the life of the believer.

There were many "conversions" in John Wesley's life and each of them involved the whole person. The warmed heart led not only to assurance but to service to the most needy of the world and an exemplary way of living.

What does holy living look like today? What are the characteristics of a person's life that qualify as marks of a radical faithfulness? Perhaps as we listen to some of Wesley's own words we will discover direction for our spiritual quest for a holy heart and holy living.

———— *Spiritual Reading* ————

Do not take part of it for the whole! What God hath joined together, put not asunder! Take no less for his religion, than the "faith that worketh by love;" all inward and outward holiness. Be not content with any religion which does not imply the destruction of all the works of the devil; that is, of all sin. We know, weakness of understanding, and a thousand infirmities, will remain, while this corruptible body remains; but sin need not remain: This is that work of the devil, eminently so called, which the Son of God was manifested to destroy in this present life. He is able, he is willing, to destroy it now, in all that believe in him . . . . Do not distrust his power, or his love! Put his promise to the proof! He hath spoken: And is he not ready likewise to perform? Only "come boldly to the throne of grace," trusting in his mercy; and you shall find, "He saveth to the uttermost all those that come to God through him!" *Sermon 62, The End of Christ's Coming, Vol. 6, p. 277*

To quicken me in making a diligent and thankful use of these peculiar advantages, I have the opportunity of communicating weekly and of public prayer twice a day. It would be easy to mention many more; as well as to show many disadvantages, which one of greater courage and skill than me, could scarce separate from the way of life you speak of. But whatever others could do, I could not. I could not stand my ground one month against intemperance in sleep, self-indulgence in food, irregularity in study; against a general lukewarmness in my affections, and remissness in my actions; against a softness directly opposite to the character of a good soldier of Jesus Christ. And then when my spirit was thus dissolved, I should be an easy prey to every temptation. Then might the cares of the world, and the desire of other things, roll back with a full tide upon me: And it would be no wonder, if while I preached to others, I myself should be a castaway. I cannot, therefore, but observe, that the question does not relate barely to the degrees of holiness, but to the very being of it. *Journal, Vol. 1, p. 179*

"But has he promised thus to save us from sin while we are in the body?" Undoubtedly he has: For a promise is implied in every commandment of God: Consequently in that, "Thou shalt love the Lord thy God with all thy heart, and with all thy soul, and with all thy mind." For this and every other commandment is given, not to the dead, but to the living. It is expressed in the words above recited, that we should walk "in holiness before him all the days of our life." *Sermon 76, On Perfection, Vol. 6, p. 418*

Yet again: His judgment concerning holiness is new. He no longer judges it to be an outward thing: To consist either in doing no harm, in doing good, or in using the ordinances of God. He sees it is the life of God in the soul; the image of God fresh stamped on the heart; an entire renewal of the mind in every temper and thought, after the likeness of Him that created it. *Journal, Vol. 1, p. 161*

Our coming to Christ ... must infer a great and mighty change. It must infer not only an *outward change,* from stealing, lying, and all corrupt communication; but a thorough *change of heart,* an *inward* renewal in the spirit of our mind. Accordingly, "the old man" implies infinitely more than outward evil conversation, even "an evil heart of unbelief," corrupted by pride and a thousand deceitful lusts. Of consequence, the "new man" must imply infinitely more than outward good conversation, even "a good heart, which after God is created in righteousness and true holiness;" a heart full of that faith which, working by love, produces all holiness of conversation. *Journal, Vol. 1, p. 214*

You never learned, either from my conversation, or preaching, or writings, that "holiness consisted in a flow of joy." I constantly told you quite the contrary: I told you it was love; the love of God and our neighbour; the image of God stamped on the heart; the life of God in the soul of man; the mind that was in Christ, enabling us to walk as Christ also walked. If Mr. Maxfield, or you, took it to be any thing else, it was your own fault, not mine. And whenever you waked out of that dream, you ought not to have laid the blame of it upon me. It is true that joy is one part of "the fruit of the Spirit," of t h e kingdom of God within us. But this is first "righteousness," then "peace," and "joy in the Holy Ghost." It is true, farther, that if you love God with "all your heart," you may "rejoice evermore." Nay it is true still farther, that many serious, humble, sober-minded believers, who do feel the love of God sometimes, and do then rejoice in God their Saviour, cannot be content with this; but pray continually, that he would enable them to love, and "rejoice in the Lord always." And no fact under heaven is more undeniable, than that God does answer this prayer; that he does, for the sake of his Son, and through the power of his Spirit, enable one and another so to do. It is also a plain fact, that this power does commonly overshadow them in an instant; and that from that time they enjoy that inward and outward holiness, to which they were utter strangers before. Possibly you might be mistaken in this; perhaps you thought you had received what you had not. But pray do not measure all men by yourself; do not imagine you are the universal standard. If you deceived yourself, (which yet I do not affirm,) you should not infer that all others do. Many think they are justified, and are not; but we cannot infer, that none are justified. So neither, if many think they are "perfected in love," and are not, will it follow that none are so. *Journal, Vol. 3, p. 341*

Thus far our Lord has been more directly employed in teaching the religion of the heart. He has shown what Christians are to be. He proceeds to show, what they are to do also: — how inward holiness is to exert itself in our outward conversation. "Blessed," saith he, "are the peace-makers; for they shall be called the children of God." *Sermon 23, Sermon on the Mount, Discourse 3, Vol. 5, p. 283*

By Methodists I mean, a people who profess to pursue (in whatsoever measure they have attained) holiness of heart and life, inward and outward conformity in all things to the revealed will of God; who place religion in an uniform resemblance of the great object of it; in a steady imitation of Him they worship, in all his imitable perfections; more particularly, in justice, mercy, and truth, or universal love filling the heart, and governing the life. *Advice to the People Called Methodists, Vol. 8, p. 352*

From long experience and observation I am inclined to think, that whoever finds redemption in the blood of Jesus, whoever is justified, has then the choice of walking in the higher or the lower path. I believe the Holy Spirit at that time sets before him the "more excellent way," and incites him to walk therein; to choose the narrowest path in the narrow way; to aspire after the heights and depths of holiness, — after the entire image of God. But if he does not accept this offer, he insensibly declines into the lower order of Christians. He still goes on in what may be called a good way, serving God in his degree, and finds mercy in the close of life, through the blood of the covenant. *Sermon 89, The More Excellent Way, Vol. 7, p. 28*

You are a new people. Your name is new, (at least, as used in a religious sense,) not heard of, till a few years ago, either in our own or any other nation. Your principles are new, in this respect, that there is no other set of people among us (and, possibly, not in the Christian world) who hold them all in the same degree and connexion; who so strenuously and continually insist on the absolute necessity of universal holiness both in heart and life; of a peaceful, joyous love of God; of a supernatural evidence of things not seen; of an inward witness that we are the children of God; and of the inspiration of the Holy Ghost, in order to any good thought, or word, or work. And perhaps there is no other set of people, (at least, not visibly united together,) who lay so much and yet no more stress than you do on rectitude of opinions, on outward modes of worship, and the use of those ordinances which you acknowledge to be of God. So much stress you lay even on right opinions, as to profess, that you earnestly desire to have a right judgment in all things, and are glad to use every means which you know or believe may be conducive thereto; and yet not so much as to condemn any man upon earth, merely for thinking otherwise than you do; much less, to imagine that God condemns him for this, if he be upright and sincere of heart. On those outward modes of worship, wherein you have been bred up, you lay so much stress as highly to approve them; but not so much as to lessen your love to those who conscientiously dissent from you herein. *Advice to the People Called Methodists, Vol. 8, p. 353*

The stated purpose of the societies was to promote "real holiness of heart and life." To this end, the meetings were designed primarily to offer mutual encouragement in the development of devotional piety based on a study of the Bible and other works of divinity, and to assist the promotion of a life of personal holiness and morality. The Orders of one society furnished a list of particular duties (and the biblical citation) which the members were expected to make "their serious endeavor" as a guide to holy living, including the following:

2. To pray many times a day, remembering our continual dependence upon God, both for spiritual and temporal things. 1 Thess. 5:17

3. To partake of the Lord's Supper at least once a month, if not prevented by a reasonable impediment. 1 Cor. 11:26, Luke 22:19

4. To practice the profoundest meekness and humility. Matt. 11:29

6. To accustom themselves to holy thoughts in all places. Psalm 2, 3

10. To shun all foreseen occasions of evil; as evil company, known temptations, etc. 1 Thess. 5:22

12. To examine themselves every night, what good or evil they have done in the day past. 2 Cor. 13:5

13. To keep a private fast once a month (especially near their approach to the Lord's Table), if at their own disposal; or to fast from some meal when they may conveniently. Matt. 6:16; Luke 5:35

14. To mortify the flesh with its affections, and lust. Gal. 5:19, 24

16. To shun spiritual pride, and the effects of it; as railing, anger, peevishness, and impatience of contradiction, etc.

18. To read pious books often for their edification

19. To be continually mindful of the great obligation of this special profession of religion, and to walk so circumspectly, that none may be offended or discouraged from it by what they see in them, nor occasion be given to any, to speak reproachfully of it.

The fellowship of the society not only supported Christian nurture, but also exercised discipline—those found to be walking "disorderly" were to be privately admonished by one or more members or, if necessary, reproved by the whole society. This inclination to reprimand immorality occasionally extended beyond the limits of the society's own small gathering into the public realm. Every member of the Cripplegate Society was to be ready to do what might be advisable "towards the punishment of publick prophaneness."

Upon this rather exclusivistic base, the societies attempted in some small measure to spread their influence within English society. The motivation for their endeavors was self-consciously circumspect—never for "popular applause or malice to any man," but rather their activities should arise out of "pure Love to God and Charity to men's souls" (J. Wickham Legg, *English Church Life from the Restoration to the Tractarian Movement*, 312).

The religious societies also encouraged certain charitable causes, for which the members subscribed regularly as their circumstances would allow. This was not the promotion of general philanthropy in the simple humanitarian sense of the word, but rather the dispensing of funds to promote more narowly the goals and purposes of the societies. Their charitable exercises were a natural outgrowth of the concern members exhibited for each other, such as visiting sick members. At a very early stage in their development, the societies began to demonstrate a special interest in the needs of the poor and disadvantaged, giving food and money to the needy, visiting the sick and imprisoned, and teaching the children of the unfortunate. *Richard Heitzenrater, Wesley and the People Called Methodists, pp. 22–23*

16

The Danger of Riches

❖— *Scripture Sentence*
> For the love of money is a root of all kinds of evil, and in their eagerness to be rich some have wandered away from the faith and pierced themselves with many pains. *1 Timothy 6:10*

❖— *Scripture Readings*

Hebrews 13:1-6
Matthew 13:18-23
Luke 18:18-30
Ezekiel 28:1-7

*1 Timothy 6:3-10
Psalm 119:1-16
Psalm 1:1-6

❖— *Silence for Meditation*

❖— *Spiritual Reading*

❖— *Recording Insights and Commitments*

❖— *Prayers of Thanks, Intercession, Petition, and Praise*

❖— *Hymn Portion*
> My talents, gifts, and graces, Lord, into thy blessed hands receive; and let me live to preach thy word, and let me to thy glory live; my every sacred moment spend in publishing the sinner's Friend. *UMH #650*

❖— *Offering All of Life to God*

❖— *Closing Affirmation*
> Truly I tell you, it will be hard for a rich person to enter the kingdom of heaven.... Then who can be saved?... For mortals it is impossible, but for God all things are possible. *Matthew 19:23-26*

——— *Reflections* ———

Many in our culture live out their lives in the fear that they will not have enough to provide for their needs to the end of life. And this fear is not entirely unfounded. There are many who do seem to miss out on the benefits of society, and who live and die with not quite enough of this world's goods. Perhaps there is reason to be concerned about how we are to live out our days, yet the scriptures suggest that being in want is not the greatest danger we face. There is something that is much more powerful and much more destructive than being in need, and that is having an abundance of this world's goods and believing they belong to us and not to God.

John Wesley was convinced that we should earn all that we can in an honorable way, and that we should save all that we can by reducing our own requirements. This was not so that his followers could store up riches, but rather so that they would have more to give to the poor and needy of the world. He was quick to observe that when the poor met Jesus Christ they became productive citizens. Living the life of faith meant a new kind of industriousness, a new kind of stewardship of time and money that invariably led to the accumulation of wealth. Rather than taking great pleasure in this, John Wesley was troubled by this remarkable transformation in the lives of those who believed and practiced their belief. He feared that as riches increased the love of riches could take the place of God. He knew the dangers of wealth.

Why Wesley saw this danger so clearly is hard to say. It could be that he himself felt the rising desire to accumulate. Perhaps he knew as well as any the desire for comfort and ease. He may have been tempted to spend what God had given in order to make himself look good. And, it may even be that underneath he too struggled with the desire to "lay up treasures" in this world—treasures adequate for any eventuality.

While Wesley may have faced the demons of riches, the most outstanding thing is the manner in which they were defeated in his preaching, teaching, and everyday life. He knew the value of money, and he knew the dangers of riches. He spent his life as a good steward of all that God gave to him. He preached, taught, and demonstrated the wisdom of living as a steward, responsible for the gift of life and all that God had added to his life. It was very clear to him that money was a wonderful gift of God and that this gift, as all others, was to be fully invested in the enterprise of God in the world. For Wesley, this meant dramatic commitment to the poor and needy and radical denial of his own desires for comfort and ease.

We live in an age and culture where commitment to the poor seems to be waning and the desire for comfort and ease has dramatically increased, fueled by a constant bombardment of advertisers trying to convince us that useless luxuries are in fact necessities. Our culture teaches us that the accumulation of wealth is of much more value than helping those less fortunate than we are. For much of society, riches have taken the place of the Living God as our number one priority and love.

Is there hope for us in such a world? Can Christians live responsibly and faithfully in a world like ours? Is it possible for us, with our riches, to inherit the kingdom of God? There is hope. We *can* live as good stewards of the gift of life and the gates of the kingdom swing wide enough for even us. But the danger of riches is real, and only by God's grace and intervention in our lives can we escape the pitfalls of wealth.

How then should we live? By first offering all that we are, have, and hope to receive to God in complete commitment. This permits us to see all things, including the gift of life, as being placed in our hands by God for a purpose and for an accounting. An examen, or self-examination, at the end of every day is a good time to bring the activities and actions of the day before God for evaluation, blessing, or correction. It is this kind of personal self-examination that can lead us to faithful decisions about the investment of our lives and our resources in the enterprise of God in the world.

One of the first words our grandchildren learned was *hot*. It was a word they were taught as they stood behind a screen and looked at the fire in the fireplace. They were taught the blessings and dangers of heat. Too much heat, or heat incorrectly channeled could be deadly. Too little was equally devastating and could also be deadly. A healthy respect for fire and heat is a part of growing up. A part of moving toward mature Christian living is a healthy respect for the danger and benefit of wealth. Is there hope for us? Of course, all things are possible with God!

O ye that have riches in possession, once more hear the word of the Lord! Ye that are rich in this world, that have food to eat, and raiment to put on, and something over, are you clear of the curse of loving the world? Are you sensible of your danger? Do you feel, "How hardly will they that have riches enter into the kingdom of heaven?" Do you continue unburned in the midst of the fire? Are you untouched with the love of the world? Are you clear from the desire of the flesh, the desire of the eyes, and the pride of life? Do you "put a knife to your throat," when you sit down to meat, lest your table should be a snare to you? Is not your belly your god? Is not eating and drinking, or any other pleasure of sense, the greatest pleasure you enjoy? Do not you seek happiness in dress, furniture, pictures, gardens, or anything else that pleases the eye? Do not you grow soft and delicate; unable to bear cold, heat, the wind or the rain, as you did when you were poor? Are you not increasing in goods, laying up treasures on earth; instead of restoring to God in the poor, not so much, or so much, but all that you can spare? Surely, "it is easier for a camel to go through the eye of a needle, than for a rich man to enter into the kingdom of heaven!" *Sermon 107, On God's Vineyard, Vol. 7, p. 212*

Desire of ease is another of these foolish and hurtful desires; desire of avoiding every cross, every degree of trouble, danger, difficulty; a desire of slumbering out life, and going to heaven (as the vulgar say) upon a feather-bed. Every one may observe how riches first beget, and then confirm and increase, this desire, making men more and more soft and delicate; more unwilling, and indeed more unable, to "take up their cross daily;" to "endure hardship as good soldiers of Jesus Christ," and to "take the kingdom of heaven by violence." *Sermon 87, The Danger of Riches, Vol. 7, p. 7*

From that express declaration of our Lord, "It is easier for a camel to go through the eye of a needle, than for a rich man to enter into the kingdom of heaven," we may easily learn, that none can *have* riches without being greatly endangered by them. But if the danger of barely having them is so great, how much greater is the danger of *increasing* them! This danger is great even to those who acquire them by their skill and industry. Therefore, nothing can be more prudent than this caution: "If riches increase, set not thine heart upon them." *Sermon 126, On the Danger of Increasing Riches, Vol. 7, p. 355*

Whoever has food to eat, and raiment to put on, with something over, is rich. Whoever has the necessaries and conveniences of life for himself and his family, and a little to spare for them that have not, is properly a rich man; unless he is a miser, a lover of money, one that hoards up what we can and ought to give to the poor. For if so, he is a poor man still, though he has millions in the bank; yea, he is the poorest of men. *Sermon 126, On the Danger of Increasing Riches, Vol. 7, p. 356*

He sent me a note, demanding the payment of one hundred pounds, which he had lent me about a year before, to pay the workmen at the Foundery. On Friday morning, at eight, he came and said, he wanted his money, and could stay no longer. I told him, I would endeavour to borrow it; and desired him to call in the evening. But he said, he could not stay so long, and must have it at twelve o clock. Where to get it, I knew not. Between nine and ten one came and offered me the use of an hundred pounds for a year. But two others had been with me before, to make the same offer. I accepted the bank note which one of them brought; and saw that God is over all! *Journal, Vol. 1, p. 393*

"The love of money," we know, "is the root of all evil;" but not the thing itself. The fault does not lie in the money, but in them that use it. It may be used ill: And what may not? But it may likewise be used well: It is full as applicable to the best, as to the worst uses. It is of unspeakable service to all civilized nations, in all the common affairs of life: It is a most compendious instrument of transacting all manner of business, and (if we use it according to Christian wisdom) of doing all manner of good. It is true, were man in a state of innocence, or were all men "filled with the Holy Ghost," so that, like the infant church at Jerusalem, "no man counted any thing he had his own," but "distribution was made to everyone as he had need," the use of it would be superseded; as we cannot conceive there is any thing of the kind among the inhabitants of heaven. But, in the present state of mankind, it is an excellent gift of God, answering the noblest ends. In the hands of his children, it is food for the hungry, drink for the thirsty, raiment for the naked: It gives to the traveller and the stranger where to lay his head. By it we may supply the place of an husband to the widow, and of a father to the fatherless. We may be a defence for the oppressed, a means of health to the sick, of ease to them that are in pain; it may be as eyes to the blind, as feet to the lame; yea, a lifter up from the gates of death! *Sermon 50, The Use of Money, Vol. 6, p. 126*

When you lay out money to please your eye, you give so much for an increase of curiosity,—for a stronger attachment to these pleasures which perish in the using. While you are purchasing anything which men use to applaud, you are purchasing more vanity. Had you not then enough of vanity, sensuality, curiosity, before? Was there need of any addition? And would you pay for it too? What manner of wisdom is this? Would not the literally throwing your money into the sea be a less mischievous folly? *Sermon 50, The Use of Money, Vol. 6, p. 132*

You see, then, what it is to "make yourselves friends of the mammon of unrighteousness," and by what means you may procure, "that when ye fail, they may receive you into the everlasting habitations." You see the nature and extent of truly Christian prudence, so far as it relates to the use of that great talent, money. Gain all you can, without hurting either yourself or your neighbour, in soul or body, by applying hereto with unintermitted diligence, and with all the understanding which God has given you;—save all you can, by cutting off every expense which serves only to indulge foolish desire; to gratify either the desire of the flesh, the desire of the eye, or the pride of life; waste nothing, living or dying, on sin or folly, whether for yourself or your children;—and then, give all you can, or, in other words, give all you have to God. Do not stint yourself ... to this or that proportion. Render unto God, not a tenth, not a third, not a half, but all that is God's, be it more or less; by employing all on yourself, your household, the household of faith, and all mankind, in such a manner, that you may give a good account of your stewardship, when ye can be no longer stewards; in such a manner, that you may give a good account of your stewardship, when ye can be no longer stewards; in such a manner as the oracles of God direct, both by general and particular precepts; in such a manner, that whatever ye do may be "a sacrifice of a sweet-smelling savour to God," and that every act may be rewarded in that day, when the Lord cometh with all his saints. *Sermon 50, The Use of Money, Vol. 6, p. 135*

I pray consider this well. Perhaps you have not seen it in this light before. When you are laying out that money in costly apparel which you could have otherwise spared for the poor, you thereby deprive them of what God, the proprietor of all, had lodged in your hands for their use. If so, what you put upon yourself, you are, in effect, tearing from the back of the naked; as the costly and delicate food which you eat, you are snatching from the mouth of the hungry. For mercy, for pity, for Christ's sake, for the honour of his gospel, stay your hand! Do not throw the money away! Do not lay out on nothing, yea, worse than nothing, what may clothe your poor, naked, shivering fellow creature! *Sermon 88, On Dress, Vol. 7, pp. 20–21*

Nearly related to anger, if not a species of it, are fretfulness and peevishness. But are the rich more assaulted by these than the poor? All experience shows that they are. One remarkable instance I was a witness of many years ago:— A gentleman of large fortune, while we were seriously conversing, ordered a servant to throw some coals on the fire: A puff of smoke came out. He threw himself back in his chair, and cried out, "O Mr. Wesley, these are the crosses which I meet with every day!" I could not help asking, "Pray, Sir John, are these the heaviest crosses you meet with?" Surely these crosses would not have fretted him so much, if he had had fifty, instead of five thousand, pounds a year! *Sermon 108, On Riches, Vol. 7, p. 20*

17

God as Loving Parent

❖— *Scripture Sentence*
> As a mother comforts her child, so I will comfort you;
> you shall be comforted. *Isaiah 66:13*

❖— *Scripture Readings*

Luke 13:31-35	Psalm 103:1-13
Psalm 68:1-6	John 12:44-50
Luke 2:41-51	*Psalm 23
Matthew 12:46-50	

❖— *Silence for Meditation*

❖— *Spiritual Reading*

❖— *Recording Insights and Commitments*

❖— *Prayers of Thanks, Intercession, Petition, and Praise*

❖— *Hymn Portion*
> There for me the Savior stands, shows his wounds
> and spreads his hands. God is love! I know, I feel;
> Jesus weeps and loves me still. *UMH #355*

❖— *Offering All of Life to God*

❖— *Closing Affirmation*
> We believe in the one true, holy and living God,
> Eternal Spirit, who is Creator, Sovereign and
> Preserver of all things visible and invisible. He is infi-
> nite in power, wisdom, justice, goodness and love,
> and rules with gracious regard for the well-being and
> salvation of all. *The Book of Discipline of The United
> Methodist Church 1996, p. 64*

Reflections

The god we worship is often too small to meet the demands of our lives, much less the demands of our violent and needy world. The Bible speaks often of a God for whom all things are possible. We all seek a God who is competent to deal with the needs of the entire creation. A god who is captive to the creation or to any other power is not God at all. The biblical witness is about a God who is omnipotent and transcendent. The Bible and Christian tradition tell of a creator God who always stands over and beyond the creation and who can never be fully comprehended by the human creature.

While such an almighty and transcendent God is part of the biblical witness, it is not the entire story. For the Bible also speaks of a God who is approachable, near, personal, loving, caring, and deeply concerned and involved with the creation. Jesus knew that God was over and above the creation, all powerful and always beyond the creature in every way. He also knew that God was personal, near, and intimately involved with the whole creation and especially humankind. Jesus knew God as caring, faithful, trustworthy, and eager to walk through life in intimate companionship with everyone who is willing to do so.

Jesus described God as a loving parent who seeks to gather humankind and hold each and all as close as a mother hen gathers and protects her chicks beneath her wings. He also described God as a waiting father, generous to all of his children who have chosen to live with him and yet anxiously seeking the lost one—never content until all have come home. The waiting father continually yearns for those who are far away and seeks them out, woos them with love, persuades them with hope, and persistently encourages their return.

These two streams of theological thought and practice are an integral part of our Methodist heritage. Methodists believe in a God for whom nothing is impossible. Therefore we are bold enough to pray for the unthinkable, from the healing of a child to the peace of the world. We are bold enough and full of enough faith to throw our every energy, our very lives, into the battle for justice and goodness. Personal and social holiness are possible only as we follow a God for whom all things are possible.

Methodists also believe in a God who is seeking relationship and companionship with each of us. God calls each of us by name and knows our most intimate secrets and our most horrible fears. And yet we are gathered in divine embrace because, as the scripture says, we have "found favor" with God. God loves us just as we are and always invites us to become more than we are. And with God's help that invitation can become reality.

Wesley believed in and preached about a God who could never be touched by evil. The God that Jesus made known is light and there is no hint of darkness, no shadow of duplicity or falsehood to be found anywhere in God's being. Therefore God could never trick, injure, or lead even one person astray. This God always means all things for good for all. Mercy and steadfast love govern every relationship with humankind and every act in history.

Because God is almighty, all knowing, all wise, and pure love, we can receive all of life as a gift from God's hand. We can make the biblical testimony our own: "It is the Lord; let him do what seems good to him" (1 Sam. 3:18). For the faithful there is no circumstance that can snatch us from the care, love, and presence of this loving parent God. We testify as did Paul, "I am convinced that neither death, nor life, nor angels, nor rulers, nor things present, nor things to come, nor powers, nor height, nor depth, nor anything else in all creation, will be able to separate us from the love of God in Christ Jesus our Lord" (Rom. 8:38-39).

As you go through the hours of this day, reflect on God as a loving parent. Remind yourself what it means to be loved, cared for, valued, found worthy, and embraced by the Divine in the experiences of your life this day. What will you attempt today because you believe in and follow a God for whom all things are possible? How will you live differently this day as you remember that God is with you, loves you, and will never permit you to be taken from that love? Following a god that is too small puts severe limits on our actions and on our confidence and self-worth. Following the God made known in Jesus Christ brings confidence, assurance, peace, joy, and hope to every disciple's life. May these gifts be yours this day and always.

——— *Spiritual Reading* ———

You, to whom I now speak, believe this love of human kind cannot spring but from the love of God. You think there can be no instance of one whose tender affection embraces every child of man, (though not endeared to him either by ties of blood, or by any natural or civil relation,) unless that affection flow from a grateful, filial love to the common Father of all; to God, considered not only as his Father, but as "the Father of the spirits of all flesh;" yea, as the general Parent and Friend of all the families both of heaven and earth. *Advice to the People Called Methodists, Vol. 8, p. 352*

How truly wise is this man! He knows himself;—an everlasting spirit, which came forth from God, and was sent down into an house of clay, not to do his own will, but the will of Him that sent him. He knows the world;—the place in which he is to pass a few days or years, not as an inhabitant, but as a stranger and sojourner, in his way to the everlasting habitations; and accordingly he uses the world as not abusing it, and as knowing the fashion of it passes away. He knows God;—his Father and his Friend, the parent of all good, the centre of the spirits of all flesh, the sole happiness of all intelligent beings. He sees, clearer than the light of the noon-day sun, that this is the end of man, to glorify Him who made him for himself, and to love and enjoy him for ever. *Sermon 33, Sermon on the Mount, Discourse 13, Vol. 5, p. 427*

In this state we were, even all mankind, when "God so loved the world, that he gave his only-begotten Son, to the end we might not perish, but have everlasting life." In the fulness of time he was made Man, another common Head of mankind, a second general Parent and Representative of the whole human race. And as such it was that "he bore our griefs," "the Lord laying upon him the iniquities of us all." Then was he "wounded for our transgressions, and bruised for our iniquities." "He made his soul an offering for sin:" He poured out his blood for the transgressors: He "bare our sins in his own body on the tree," that by his stripes we might be healed: And by that one oblation of himself, once offered, he hath redeemed me and all mankind; having thereby "made a full, perfect, and sufficient sacrifice for the sins of the whole world." *Sermon 5, Justification by Faith, Vol. 5, p. 55*

We may learn from hence, in the Third place, what is the proper nature of religion, of the religion of Jesus Christ. It is *therapeia psuches*, God's method of healing a soul which is thus diseased. Hereby the great Physician of souls applies medicines to heal this sickness; to restore human nature, totally corrupted in all its faculties. God heals all our Atheism by the knowledge of Himself, and of Jesus Christ whom he hath sent; by giving us faith, a divine evidence and conviction of God, and of the things of God, — in particular, of this important truth, "Christ loved me, and gave himself for me." By repentance and lowliness of heart, the deadly disease of pride is healed; that of selfwill by resignation, a meek and thankful submission to the will of God; and for the love of the world in all its branches, the love of God is the sovereign remedy. Now, this is properly religion, "faith" thus "working by love;" working the genuine meek humility, entire deadness to the world, with a loving thankful acquiescence in, and conformity to, the whole will and word of God. *Sermon 44, Original Sin, Vol. 6, p. 64*

Holiness is another of the attributes of the almighty, allwise God. He is infinitely distant from every touch of evil. He "is light; and in him is no darkness at all." He is a God of unblemished justice and truth; but above all is his mercy. This we may easily learn from that beautiful passage in the thirty-third and fourth chapters of Exodus: "And Moses said, I beseech thee, show me thy glory. And the Lord descended in the cloud, and proclaimed the name of the Lord,—The Lord, The Lord God, merciful and gracious, longsuffering, and abundant in goodness and truth, keeping mercy for thousands, and forgiving iniquity and transgressions and sin." *Sermon 114, The Unity of the Divine Being, Vol. 7, p. 266*

From hence it manifestly appears, what is the nature of the new birth. It is that great change which God works in the soul when he brings it into life; when he raises it from the death of sin to the life of righteousness. It is the change wrought in the whole soul by the almighty Spirit of God when it is "created anew in Christ Jesus;" when it is "renewed after the image of God, in righteousness and true holiness;" when the love of the world is changed into the love of God; pride into humility; passion into meekness; hatred, envy, malice, into a sincere, tender, disinterested love for all mankind. In a word, it is that change whereby the earthly, sensual, devilish mind is turned into the "mind which was in Christ Jesus." This is the nature of the new birth: "So is every one that is born of the Spirit." *Sermon 45, The New Birth, Vol. 6, p. 71*

O the tender care of Almighty God in bringing up his children! How are we bound to love so indulgent a Father, and to fall down in wonder and adoration of his great and glorious name, for his tender mercies! *Journal, Vol. 1, p. 478*

In the morning, being by myself, I found the work of the Spirit was very powerful upon me: (Although you know God does not deal with every soul in the same way:) As my mother bore me with great pain, so did I feel great pain in my soul in being born of God. Indeed I thought the pains of death were upon me, and that my soul was then taking leave of the body. I thought I was going to Him whom I saw with strong faith standing ready to receive me. In this violent agony I continued about four hours; and then I began to feel the "Spirit of God bearing witness with my spirit, that I was born of God." Because I was a child of God, He "sent forth the Spirit of his Son into me, crying, Abba, Father." For that is the cry of every new-born soul. O mighty, powerful, happy change! I who had nothing but devils ready to drag me to hell, now found I had angels to guard me to my reconciled Father; and my Judge, who just before stood ready to condemn me, was now become my righteousness. But I cannot express what God hath done for my soul. No; this is to be my everlasting employment when I have put off this frail, sinful body, when I join with that great multitude which no man can number, in singing praises to the Lamb that loved us, and gave himself for us! O how powerful are the workings of the Almighty in a new born soul! The love of God was shed abroad in my heart, and a flame kindled there, so that my body was almost torn asunder. *Journal, Vol. 1, p. 168*

For Wesley ... the first "Person" of the Godhead relates to humanity as Creator/Sustainer, Provider, Governor/Judge, and Physician. The identification of these functions is hardly novel in the Christian tradition, although the fourth is less common than the others. If there is anything distinctive in Wesley's treatment, it is his interrelation of the four.

... Wesley's defining model for understanding God was more that of a loving parent than of a sovereign monarch. This suggestion seems consistent with his convictions about the work of God/Father. The dimensions of God's work as Creator and Governor are easily appropriated with a defining model of sovereign monarch. When the dimensions of Provider and Physician are integrated with these, however, a beneficent tone is added which is more typical of familial settings than regal ones.

A parental model of God is particularly appropriate if, as I am inclined to think, Physician and Provider are the dimensions of God's work that Wesley valued most. As evidence I would point to his sermon on "God's Love to Fallen Man," where he argues that if humanity had not fallen, we would never have had the wound for whose healing Christ had to take our nature. He then concludes that without the Fall we would have known God as Creator, Preserver, and Governor; but not under the "nearest and dearest relation of delivering up his Son for us all." That is, we would not have known God as the one *providing healing* for our wound.

The resulting focus of Wesley's understanding of God is perhaps best seen in his suggestion for how a parent can explain God to a child:

> God (though you cannot see him) is above the sky, and is a deal brighter than the sun! It is he, it is God, that made the sun, and you and me, and everything. It is he that makes the grass and the flowers grow; that makes the trees green, and the fruit to come upon them! Think what he can do! He can do whatever he pleases. He can strike me or you dead in a moment. But he loves you; he loves to do you good. He loves to make you happy. Should not you then love him! You

love me, because I love you and do you good. But it is God that makes me love you. Therefore, you should love him. *[Sermon 94, On Family Religion, III. 7, Works, 3:341]*

Note how this explanation touches briefly on Creator and Governor dimensions of God, but moves to Provider and parental images in the main point.

Also evident in the preceding quotation are the numerous masculine pronouns for God. Wesley followed traditional Christian practice in calling the first "Person" of the Godhead "Father." However, his reasons were more than merely traditional. The claim that God was not a dispassionate, aloof Sovereign but a protecting, providing Father was central to his conception of the Christian faith. Of course, given his recognition of the analogical nature of God-language, the primary issue here was not God's sex, but God's personal and caring character; as he commented on the opening of the Lord's Prayer, "if [God] is a Father, then he is good, then he is loving to his children."

It is suggestive in this regard that Wesley could also refer to God as "Parent." All the same, there is little evidence that he used consciously maternal or female images for God—even though there was biblical warrant to do so. Whatever his relative sensitivity to the inclusive nature of God, Wesley remained a man of his context. *Randy L. Maddox, Responsible Grace, pp. 63–64*

18

Salvation by Faith

❖— *Scripture Sentence*
Restore to me the joy of your salvation, and sustain in me a willing spirit. *Psalm 51:12*

❖— *Scripture Readings*

Philippians 2:1-12	Acts 4:1-12
Luke 2:22-35	Luke 19:1-10
*1 Peter 1:3-9	2 Corinthians 6:1-10
1 Thessalonians 5:1-11	

❖— *Silence for Meditation*

❖— *Spiritual Reading*

❖— *Recording Insights and Commitments*

❖— *Prayers of Thanks, Intercession, Petition, and Praise*

❖— *Hymn Portion*
Let us plead for faith alone, faith which by our works is shown; God it is who justifies, only faith the grace applies. *UMH #385*

❖— *Offering All of Life to God*

❖— *Closing Affirmation*
Surely God is my salvation; I will trust, and will not be afraid, for the Lord God is my strength and my might; he has become my salvation. *Isaiah 12:2*

—— Reflections ——

The reward system is operative in almost every enterprise and relationship in our western culture. Work hard, get a raise. Study hard, get good grades. Be extra nice and grandpa may give you a dollar. Smile and you may get a large tip. To get ahead one has to jump through the appropriate hoops. Everywhere we turn, the reward system is firmly in place. It is difficult to imagine God's unconditional love and grace that reach out to us and offer salvation without cost. It seems too good to be true. God's gracious offer of salvation in this world and the next, and our own faith, is all it takes to receive salvation? Hard to believe. And yet John Wesley, along with all the other giants of the church, proclaimed this message.

Salvation by faith means that no one is excluded from the Table of the Lord. The heavenly banquet is spread for all and none is prevented from participation. Social, political, financial, physical, and educational requirements often determine where we can gain entrance in this world; but not so in the Kingdom of God. Here, all are wanted and welcome. Here the only requirement is desire for the gift and faith to receive it.

Wesley was convinced that salvation was more than just being seated at the heavenly banquet, although it did include that. For him salvation encompassed all of life, including deliverance from the bondage of sin and enjoyment of the fruits of faithfulness in this life, as well as life in the world to come. For Wesley salvation was not of our doing but completely a gift from God. Without God's gracious call and generous offer we could never even respond. Salvation is a gift of God, initiated by God and completed by God. Even the faith to receive salvation is a gift.

Although faith is the only requirement for salvation, Wesley was convinced that saving faith had some consequences. These consequences could be observed and evaluated. Saving faith resulted in acts of mercy, compassion, devotion, and witness. While these acts were not requirements for salvation, they were signs of salvation. God works with the faithful to at once begin living within the Kingdom of God. Salvation means the incorporation of the ways of God into one's daily life as surely as it means forgiveness of sin and assurance of eternal reward.

Wesley believed that salvation begins with God and ends

with God; salvation is lived out in this life and the next. He proclaimed that God sought to welcome every human being home—home to communion, fellowship, and companionship with God. And this homecoming did not wait until death. It began in this life and carried over into the life to come.

We are all invited to receive this gift. We do not have to become good enough first and we do not have to demonstrate our faithfulness first. We may receive the gift of salvation by faith just as we are. That gift includes assurance of sin forgiven, assurance of companionship with God in this life, and confidence of our place in those "rooms" prepared by Jesus for the faithful.

While we may *receive* the gift just as we are, we do not *stay* just as we are. Salvation by faith leads to acts of mercy, justice, compassion, witness, and piety. These are all means of grace, ways that God offers to us to stay centered in the life of the spirit. They are not requirements for entrance into salvation but they are requirements for those who wish to live the redeemed life.

Are you plagued with the evils of the world and your inability to make a difference? Do you wonder about sin and forgiveness? Deep down inside do you believe you have to do something good before God can really love you? Do you sometimes wonder about your place in God's eternal kingdom? Most of us would have to answer yes to one or more of these simple questions. And yet, our Wesleyan heritage proclaims that we are loved just as we are, that our lives do matter and each one of us can make an important difference, that we need not carry guilt for the past, and that today we may begin living a life in God's kingdom. The remedy for the sickness of humankind is called *salvation*.

When we receive and reflect upon the gift of salvation it is natural and appropriate to take time to listen to what is being awakened within us. We may be prompted to a new life of prayer. We may be urged to a new life of witness. We may be directed to a place of service that we had never seen before. We may be drawn deeper into our inner spiritual life and driven outward to a more active involvement with the world around us. Salvation is available just as we are and always leads us to become more than we are.

I began preaching this new doctrine, though my soul started back from the work. The first person to whom I offered salvation by faith alone, was a prisoner under sentence of death. His name was Clifford. Peter Bohler had many times desired me to speak to him before. But I could not prevail on myself so to do; being still (as I had been many years) a zealous assertor of the impossibility of a death-bed repentance. *Journal, Vol. 1, p. 86*

I preached in the morning at St. Ann's Aldersgate; and in the afternoon at the Savoy chapel, free salvation by faith in the blood of Christ. I was quickly apprized, that at St. Ann's, likewise, I am to preach no more. *Journal, Vol. 1, p. 95*

After we had wandered many years in the *new path*, of salvation by *faith* and *works*; about two years ago it pleased God to show us the *old way*, of salvation by *faith* only. And many soon tasted of this salvation, "being justified freely, having peace with God, rejoicing in hope of the glory of God," and having his "love shed abroad in their hearts." These now ran the way of his commandments: They performed all their duty to God and man. They walked in all the ordinances of the Lord; and through these means, which he had appointed for that end, received daily grace to help in time of need, and went on from faith to faith. *Journal, Vol. 1, p. 275*

If then sinful men find favour with God, it is "grace upon grace!" If God vouchsafe still to pour fresh blessings upon us, yea, the greatest of all blessings, salvation; what can we say to these things, but, "Thanks be unto God for his unspeakable gift!" And thus it is. Herein "God commendeth his love toward us, in that, while we were yet sinners, Christ died" to save us. "By grace," then, "are ye saved through faith." Grace is the source, faith the condition, of salvation. *Sermon 1, Salvation by Faith, Vol. 5, p. 8*

Ye are saved (to comprise all in one word) from sin. This is the salvation which is through faith. This is that great salvation foretold by the angel, before God brought his First-begotten into the world: "Thou shalt call his name JESUS: For he shall save his people from their sins." And neither here, nor in other parts of holy writ, is there any limitation or restriction. All his people, or, as it is elsewhere expressed, "all that believe in him," he will save from all their sins; from original and actual, past and present sin, "of the flesh and of the spirit." Through faith that is in him, they are saved both from the guilt and from the power of it. *Sermon 1, Salvation by Faith, Vol. 5, p. 10*

For by grace are ye saved through faith; and that not of yourselves. Of yourselves cometh neither your faith nor your salvation: It is the gift of God; the free, undeserved gift; the faith through which ye are saved, as well as the salvation, which he of his own good pleasure, his mere favour, annexes thereto. That ye believe, is one instance of his grace; that, believing, ye are saved, another. Not of works, lest any man should boast. For all our works, all our righteousness, which were before our believing, merited nothing of God but condemnation: So far were they from deserving faith, which therefore, whenever given, is not of works. Neither is salvation of the works we do when we believe: For it is then God that worketh in us: And, therefore, that he giveth us a reward for what he himself worketh, only commendeth the riches of his mercy, but leaveth us nothing whereof to glory. *Sermon 1, Salvation by Faith, Vol. 5, p. 13*

By the same faith we feel the power of Christ every moment resting upon us, whereby alone we are what we are; whereby we are enabled to continue in spiritual life, and without which, notwithstanding all our present holiness, we should be devils in the next moment. But as long as we retain our faith in him, we "draw water out of the wells of salvation." Leaning on our Beloved, even Christ in us the hope of glory, who dwelleth in our hearts by faith, who likewise is ever interceding for us at the right hand of God, we receive help from him to think, and speak, and act, what is acceptable in his sight. Thus does he "prevent" them that believe, in all their "doings, and further them with his continual help;" so that all their designs, conversations, and actions are "begun, continued, and ended in him." Thus doth he, "cleanse the thoughts of their hearts, by the inspiration of his Holy Spirit, that they may perfectly love him, and worthily magnify his holy name." *Sermon 14, The Repentance of Believers, Vol. 5, p. 167*

Hear ye this, all you that are called Methodists! You, of all men living, are most concerned herein. You constantly speak of salvation by faith: And you are in the right for so doing. You maintain, (one and all,) that a man is justified by faith without the works of the law. And you cannot do otherwise, without giving up the Bible, and betraying your own souls. You insist upon it, that we are saved by faith: And, undoubtedly, so we are. But consider, meantime, that let us have ever so much faith, and be our faith ever so strong, it will never save us from hell, unless it now save us from all unholy tempers, from pride, passion, impatience; from all arrogance of spirit, all haughtiness and overbearing; from wrath, anger, bitterness; from discontent, murmuring, fretfulness, peevishness. *Sermon 91, On Charity, Vol. 7, p. 54*

Now, if by salvation we mean a present salvation from sin, we cannot say, holiness is the condition of it; for it is the thing itself. Salvation, in this sense, and holiness, are synonymous terms. We must therefore say, "We are saved by faith." Faith is the sole condition of this salvation. For without faith we cannot be thus saved. But whosoever believeth is saved already. *A Farther Appeal to Men of Reason and Religion, Vol. 8, p. 47*

Sometimes He acts on the wills and affections of men; withdrawing them from evil, inclining them to good, inspiring (breathing, as it were) good thoughts into them: So it has frequently been expressed, by an easy, natural metaphor, strictly analogous to *ruach, pneuma, spiritus,* and the words used in most modern tongues also, to denote the third person in the ever-blessed Trinity. But however it be expressed, it is certain all true faith, and the whole work of salvation, every good thought, word, and work, is altogether by the operation of the Spirit of God. *A Farther Appeal to Men of Reason and Religion, Vol. 8, p. 49*

Wesley called upon his preachers to "preach the whole gospel, even justification and sanctification, preparatory to glory." This call suggests again Wesley's practical-theological concern for the proper formation of his people. Also evident is a distinction between three dimensions of human salvation. Wesley's most explicit delineation of these three dimensions was pardon—salvation begun, holiness—salvation continued, and heaven—salvation finished. Some other common threefold formulations were justification, sanctification, and consummation; or pardon, grace, and glory. To suggest an alliteration, Wesley understood human salvation in its fullest sense to include deliverance (1) immediately from the penalty of sin, (2) progressively from the plague of sin, and (3) eschatologically from the very presence of sin and its effects. *Randy L. Maddox, Responsible Grace, p. 143*

Wesley's famous description of the Aldersgate event culminates in the claim that then he sensed that Christ had "taken away *my* sins, even *mine*, and saved me from the law of sin and death." It is sometimes assumed that Wesley was making here only a juridical claim that he was aware of God's pardon of the *penalty* of his sin. He was actually claiming more than this, because he had come to Aldersgate Street on the evening of May 24 expecting much more than this!

The driving passion of Wesley's life prior to 1738 had been to conquer the *plague* of sin and be conformed to the model of Christ. Peter Bohler had recently persuaded him that this deliverance could happen instantaneously by simple faith, in conjunction with his assurance of God's forgiveness. On the morning of May 24 he found his attention drawn to two Scripture verses: 2 Peter 1:4, which he took as a direct promise that he could *be* a partaker of the Divine nature; and Mark 12:34, which raised his expectation that this would happen very soon. In worship that afternoon he was struck by the words of the anthem which called for trust in God to provide mercy *and* redemption from all one's sins. Finally, the reading from Luther at Aldersgate Street that night placed as much stress on God's grace giving us a new heart that would incessantly do good works as it did on forgiveness. Against this background, what Wesley hoped for—and initially claimed—at Aldersgate was *full* salvation from *both* the penalty and the plague of sin! *Randy L. Maddox, Responsible Grace, p. 144*

19

Justifying Grace

❖— *Scripture Sentence*
   For the grace of God has appeared, bringing salvation to all. *Titus 2:11*

❖— *Scripture Readings*

   Romans 5:1-11   *Ephesians 2:1-10
   Romans 5:12-21   1 Peter 4:1-11
   Galatians 2:15-21   Luke 18:18-30
   Acts 15:1-11

❖— *Silence for Meditation*

❖— *Spiritual Reading*

❖— *Recording Insights and Commitments*

❖— *Prayers of Thanks, Intercession, Petition, and Praise*

❖— *Hymn Portion*
   We by his Spirit prove and know the things of God,
   the things which freely of his love he hath on us
   bestowed. Our nature's turned, our mind transformed in all its powers, and both the witnesses are
   joined, the Spirit of God with ours. *UMH #372*

❖— *Offering All of Life to God*

❖— *Closing Affirmation*
   Indeed, God did not send the Son into the world to
   condemn the world, but in order that the world
   might be saved through him. *John 3:17*

Reflections

Everything is for sale today. If you have enough money, you can buy anything. Everyone has a price. If you don't have it and want it, buy it. These are common expressions, and they reflect the belief and practice of many around the world. That belief maintains that all things are for sale to those who have the necessary resources.

This concept is not limited to the secular world but has invaded the life of the church in some very profound ways. We often teach and are taught that the cost of discipleship is severe and that faithful Christians practice what the Sermon on the Mount proclaims. There is ample evidence that this is true. So, it is easy to take the next step to believing that we can, by our good works, earn salvation. If we are just good enough, do enough, deny ourselves enough, we will be forgiven, redeemed, and reconciled to God. Following this path brings no peace, assurance, or sense of companionship with God. Rather than asking why we are miserable and have no deep peace and joy in our relationship with God, we just try harder to earn our way to companionship with God. We do this through busyness in the church, prayer, or acts of compassion in the world. We are led to believe that if we work hard enough, salvation will be ours.

But the biblical view of life is quite different and John Wesley, grounded as he was in the Bible, was certain that salvation was not for sale. He was convinced that no one could ever earn a place at God's table. No one was good enough or faithful enough to deserve the gift of salvation. There was a great barrier between the Holy God and sinful humankind—a barrier that humankind could not overcome. But God took the initiative and not only crossed the barrier, but through the life, death, and resurrection of Jesus Christ, destroyed every barrier, reconciling humankind to God.

There seems to be a human tendency to try and justify ourselves. We like to compare ourselves to those whose lives, in our view, are less moral or faithful than our own. It is not uncommon to hear political leaders and little children alike blame others for their condition or actions. While deep within we know we are not "good enough," we nevertheless try to justify ourselves. John Wesley had every reason to follow this line of thought. Growing up in the Anglican tradition, he was taught, and early in his life believed, that the way to salvation was found in a high morality and an abundance of good works. After all, these were (and still are) expected marks of a Christian. But he soon learned that this was an inadequate foundation for Christian theology and for the Christian life. If we were required to earn our way to God we were without hope. However, the remedy was offered for our sin and rebellion; that remedy was faith in God's grace that reached out to all with the offer of justification, reconciliation, and restoration.

In his sermon "Salvation by Faith," Wesley declared, "This then is the salvation which is through faith; a salvation from sin, and the consequences of sin, both often expressed in the word *justification.* . . ."

We can never justify ourselves, be reconciled to God, or earn our way to heaven on our own. But the marvelous good news is that God offers it all to us as gift. We are saved, in this world and the next, by grace through faith. We are justified, our loving relationship with God is restored, by God's action and not our own. The apostle Paul put it this way, "Wretched man that I am! Who will rescue me from this body of death? Thanks be to God through Jesus Christ our Lord." What can we do to earn our salvation? Nothing! And yet a natural response to God's gracious gift is to give thanks and to determine to walk in harmony with God and God's way.

——— *Spiritual Reading* ———

But when we have once received this Spirit of adoption, this "peace which passes all understanding," and which expels all painful doubt and fear, will "keep our hearts and minds in Christ Jesus." And when this has brought forth its genuine fruit, all inward and outward holiness, it is undoubtedly the will of Him that calleth us, to give us always what he has once given; so that there is no need that we should ever more be deprived of either the testimony of God's Spirit, or the testimony of our own, the consciousness of our walking in all righteousness and true holiness. *Sermon 11, The Witness of the Spirit, Vol. 5, p. 134*

When I met Peter Bohler again, he consented to put the dispute upon the issue which I desired, namely Scripture and experience. I first consulted the Scripture. But when I set aside the glosses of men, and simply considered the words of God, comparing them together, endeavouring to illustrate the obscure by the plainer passages; I found that they all made against me, and was forced to retreat to my last hold, "that experience would never agree with the *literal interpretation* of those scriptures. Nor could I therefore allow it to be true, till I found some living witnesses of it." He replied, he could show me such at any time; if I desired it, the next day. And accordingly, the next day he came again with three others, all of whom testified, of their own personal experience, that a true living faith in Christ is inseparable from a sense of pardon for all past, and freedom from all present, sins. They added with one mouth, that this faith was the gift, the free gift of God; and that he would surely bestow it upon every soul who earnestly and perseveringly sought it. I was now thoroughly convinced; and, by the grace of God, I resolved to seek it unto the end, 1. By absolutely renouncing all dependence, in whole or in part, upon my own works or righteousness; on which I had really grounded my hope of salvation, though I knew it not, from my youth up. 2. By adding to the constant use of all the other means of grace, continual prayer for this very thing, justifying, saving faith, a full reliance on the blood of Christ shed for me; a trust in Him, as my Christ, as my sole justification, sanctification, and redemption. *Journal, Vol. 1, p. 102*

Thus look unto Jesus! There is the Lamb of God, who taketh away thy sins! Plead thou no works, no righteousness of thine own! no humility, contrition, sincerity! In nowise. That were, in very deed, to deny the Lord that bought thee. No: Plead thou, singly, the blood of the covenant, the ransom paid for thy proud, stubborn, sinful soul. Who art thou, that now seest and feelest both thine inward and outward ungodliness? Thou art the man! I want thee for my Lord! I challenge *thee* for a child of God by faith! The Lord hath need of thee. Thou who feelest thou art just fit for hell, art just fit to advance his glory; the glory of his free grace, justifying the ungodly and him that worketh not. O come quickly! Believe in the Lord Jesus; and thou, even thou, art reconciled to God. *Sermon 5, Justification by Faith, Vol. 5, p. 64*

I showed at large, 1. That the Lord's Supper was ordained by God, to be a means of conveying to men either preventing, or justifying, or sanctifying grace, according to their several necessities. 2. That the persons for whom it was ordained, are all those who know and feel that they want the grace of God, either to restrain them from sin, or to show their sins forgiven, or to renew their souls in the image of God. 3. That inasmuch as we come to his table, not to give him any thing, but to receive whatsoever he sees best for us, there is no previous preparation indispensably necessary, but a desire to receive whatsoever he pleases to give. And, 4. That no fitness is required at the time of communicating, but a sense of our state, of our utter sinfulness and helplessness; every one who knows he is fit for hell, being just fit to come to Christ, in this as well as all other ways of his appointment. *Journal, Vol. 1, p. 280*

Yet, Thirdly, several of these, after being thoroughly sensible of their fall, and deeply ashamed before God, have been again filled with his love, and not only perfected therein, but stablished, strengthened, and settled. They have received the blessing they had before with abundant increase. Nay, it is remarkable, that many who had fallen either from justifying or from sanctifying grace, and so deeply fallen that they could hardly be ranked among the servants of God, have been restored (but seldom till they had been shaken, as it were, over the mouth of hell,) and that very frequently in an instant, to all that they had lost. They have, at once, recovered both a consciousness of his favour, and the experience of the pure love of God. In one moment they received anew both remission of sins, and a lot among them that were sanctified. *Sermon 86, A Call to Backsliders, Vol. 6, p. 526*

THAT great truth, "that we are saved by faith," will never be worn out; and that sanctifying as well as justifying faith is the free gift of God. Now, with God one day is as a thousand years. It plainly follows, that the quantity of time is nothing to Him: Centuries, years, months, days, hours, and moments are exactly the same. Consequently, he can as well sanctify in a day after we are justified, as a hundred years. There is no difference at all, unless we suppose Him to be such a one as ourselves. Accordingly we see, in fact, that some of the most unquestionable witnesses of sanctifying grace were sanctified within a few days after they were justified. I have seldom known so devoted a soul as S— H—, at Macclesfield, who was sanctified within nine days after she was convinced of sin. She was then twelve years old, and I believe was never afterwards heard to speak an improper word, or known to do an improper thing. Her look struck an awe into all that saw her. She is now in Abraham's bosom. *Letter to Mrs. A. F., Vol. 12, p. 333*

Proceed we now to the Second point: If God worketh in you, then work out your own salvation. The original word, rendered *work out,* implies the doing a thing thoroughly. *Your own;* for you yourselves must do this, or it will be left undone for ever. Your *own salvation:* Salvation begins with what is usually termed (and very properly) *preventing grace;* including the first wish to please God,—the first dawn of light concerning his will, and the first slight transient conviction of having sinned against him. All these imply some tendency toward life; some degree of salvation; the beginning of a deliverance from a blind, unfeeling heart, quite insensible of God and the things of God. Salvation is carried on by *convincing grace,* usually in Scripture termed *repentance;* which brings a larger measure of self-knowledge, and a farther deliverance from the heart of stone. Afterwards we experience the proper Christian salvation; whereby, "through grace," we "are saved by faith;" consisting of these two grand branches, justification and sanctification. By justification we are saved from the guilt of sin and restored to the favour of God; by sanctification we are saved from the power and root of sin, and restored to the image of God. All experience, as well as Scripture, show this salvation to be both instantaneous and gradual. It begins the moment we are justified, in the holy, humble, gentle, patient love of God and man. It gradually increases from that moment, as "a grain of mustard seed, which, at first, is the least of all seeds," but afterwards puts forth large branches, and becomes a great tree; till, in another instant, the heart is cleansed from all sin, and filled with pure love to God and man. But even that love increases more and more, till we "grow up in all things into Him that is our Head;" till we attain "the measure of the stature of the fulness of Christ." *Sermon 85, On Working Out Our Own Salvation, Vol. 6, p. 509*

"However, may not the speaking thus of the mercy of God, as saving or justifying freely by faith only, encourage men in sin?" Indeed it may and will: Many will "continue in sin that grace may abound:" But their blood is upon their own head. The goodness of God ought to lead them to repentance; and so it will those who are sincere of heart. When they know there is yet forgiveness with him, they will cry aloud that he would blot out their sins also, through faith which is in Jesus. And if they earnestly cry, and faint not; if they seek him in all the means he hath appointed; if they refuse to be comforted till he come; "he will come, and will not tarry." *Sermon 1, Salvation by Faith, Vol. 5, p. 13*

Justification by grace through faith was a central motif in John Wesley's thought. He was emphatic: Salvation is the work of God. Salvation is a gracious gift of God and it must not be confused with human achievement, with the exercise of human will, or with the faithful pursuit of a Christian style of life. Salvation is the work of God and of no other; justification is by grace. . . .

It is significant that in Wesley's arrangement of his sermons, the very first is "Salvation by Faith." In this homily he stressed that a person's salvation is totally dependent upon God's free unmerited grace. He wrote, "Grace is the source; faith is the condition of salvation." And, "It is this doctrine, which our

Church justly calls *the strong rock and foundation of the Christian religion." Thomas A. Langford, Practical Divinity, pp. 27–28*

In the sermon "Salvation by Faith," he presented the meaning of justification.

> This then is the salvation which is through faith, even in the present world: a salvation from sin, and the consequences of sin, both often expressed in the word *justification*; which, taken in the largest sense, implies a deliverance fom guilt and punishment, by the atonement of Christ actually applied to the soul of the sinner now believing on him, and a deliverance from the whole body of sin, through Christ formed in his heart. So that he who is thus justified, or saved by faith, is *indeed* born again.

The key phrases in this statement are "the present world," "deliverance," and "born again." So justification is an actual deliverance from sin in present life; it issues into a new birth which begins maturation into the fullness of Christian living. Wesley's consistent central theme was salvation by faith—beginning in repentance and developing into a new life of holy living. *Thomas A. Langford, Practical Divinity, p. 29*

Justification is by grace through faith; grace makes faith a possibility, for faith is a graciously enabled response to grace. In this sense, "Faith, therefore, is the *necessary* condition of justification; yes, the *only necessary* condition thereof." . . .

Faith, as Wesley defined it, is trust and confidence. It is response to the initiative of God. Human beings who were estranged from God are now, by forgiveness, drawn into positive relationship, a relationship with fulfilled meaning. Faith is knowledge of God, as God has prepared the way for and now prompts human response. . . .

The source of faith is God. Wesley spoke of faith as "a divine supernatural ἔλεγκος *evidence or conviction,* 'of things not seen,' not discoverable by our bodily senses, as being either past, future, or spiritual." There is no self-salvation. Justification is a free gift, the gift of God in Jesus Christ; and faith, the condition of justification, also is a gift given to fallen persons. *Thomas A. Langford, Practical Divinity, pp. 30–31*

20

The Way to Heaven

❖— *Scripture Sentence*
They desire a better country, that is, a heavenly one.
Therefore God is not ashamed to be called their God;
indeed, he has prepared a city for them.
Hebrews 11:16

❖— *Scripture Readings*

2 Peter 3:11-18   Luke 10:25-37
*John 14:1-7   Romans 2:1-11
1 Peter 3:13-22   Romans 5:12-21
1 Peter 4:7-19

❖— *Silence for Meditation*

❖— *Spiritual Reading*

❖— *Recording Insights and Commitments*

❖— *Prayers of Thanks, Intercession, Petition, and Praise*

❖— *Hymn Portion*
Come, let us join our friends above who have
obtained the prize, and on the eagle wings of love to
joys celestial rise. Let saints on earth unite to sing
with those to glory gone, for all the servants of our
King in earth and heaven are one. *UMH #709*

❖— *Offering All of Life to God*

❖— *Closing Affirmation*
Whoever serves me must follow me, and where I am,
there will my servant be also. Whoever serves me,
the Father will honor. *John 12:26*

Reflections

Heaven is not taken very seriously in our time. Even church members hear few sermons on the reality of salvation that includes eternity. The editor of a well known magazine was invited to speak to an annual meeting of priests, and his address was about heaven. When asked why he chose such a topic, he responded, "It became clear to me that if I wanted to hear a lecture on heaven, I would have to give it myself." We don't hear much preaching and even less serious discussion about heaven in or out of the church.

There may be an underlying fear that we will be considered "other worldly" and not relevant to this world if we speak of heaven. Our desire to make this world better may have blinded us to the truth that we are, like John Wesley, "a creature of a day, passing through life as an arrow through the air." Life in this world is getting longer for some but it is certain to end for all. For most, life in this world will be too short. For others, there may be the conviction that this life is all there is. The salvation promised and described in scripture and taught by Jesus saw all of life as one piece and never ending. The transition from this life to the next was seen as natural. As Wesley said, "I am a spirit come from God and returning to God." For him the evidence was too great to overlook and too formidable to deny.

While the way to heaven may not hold much interest for us, it did for John Wesley. He said, "I want to know one thing ... the way to heaven." He believed that it was God's intention for us to live in full companionship with God in this world and the next. For him salvation included this world and the next. He believed that God gave us careful instruction in the Bible so that we could each travel the way to heaven and claim this gift of full salvation for ourselves.

John Wesley integrated salvation in this world and the next in his preaching, teaching, and daily living. The two could not be separated. To receive the gift of salvation in this world was to receive the gift of salvation in the world to come. To walk in faithfulness with God in this world was to walk with God in faithfulness in the next world. And to walk in faithfulness with God was the way to know the assurance and joy of salvation now and for eternity.

Salvation results in a new relationship with God. Sinners find themselves reconciled to the One in whose sight all sin is committed. This new relationship offers great benefits and demands radical response. A gift so great could not be shrugged off and forgotten. The response to the gift of salvation that early Methodists taught and practiced was holy living. To know of and to experience the love of God ignited a response that invaded all of life. At the center of this response was love for God and love for neighbor that resulted in a balanced holy life that included social and personal holiness.

Many years ago now, my young son and I were doing some shopping in a department store that was being visited by a large number of persons from a local religious community. As we left the store, my son said, "Dad, why do they all look so sad?" I couldn't answer because I didn't know. As I have observed the church, I have sometimes asked the same question. With the salvation offered, why are we so sad?

Could it be that we have overlooked the companionship of the living God in our daily lives and rejected the reality of life that is eternal? What would our lives be like if we had a bone deep conviction that we have come from God, now live with God, and will go to God when we die? Would our anxiety and stress be reduced? Would our priorities shift? Would we embark on an intentional life of holiness? I believe the answer is an unqualified yes.

Persons who know that their lives are authored, created by God can live "at home" and "at peace" in the world that God has created. They can live, as Walter Brueggemann says, "authorized lives." To know that we have come from God, live with God, and are going to God is to live a life of confidence and assurance. Not only death but life has lost its fearfulness. Tragedy may overtake us and shake us but it cannot snatch us from the hand of the One who made us, sustains us, and even now prepares for our transition to a richer, fuller life of companionship in paradise (Luke 23:43).

Christians at their best look life and death full in the face without fear because they know to whom they belong and where they are going. Wesley believed that everyone was on the way to somewhere. He wanted to be on the way to heaven, and he was confident that this way was made clear in the biblical witness. His determination to travel this way led to a remarkable life of faithfulness. We are all on the way to somewhere and are always invited to be on the way to God, in this life and the next.

—— *Spiritual Reading* ——

I have accordingly set down in the following sermons what I find in the Bible concerning the way to heaven; with a view to distinguish this way of God from all those which are the invention of men. I have endeavoured to describe the true, the scriptural, experimental religion, so as to omit nothing which is a real part thereof, and to add nothing thereto which is not. And herein it is more especially my desire, First to guard those who are just setting their faces toward heaven, (and who, having little acquaintance with the things of God, are the more liable to be turned out of the way,) from formality, from mere outside religion, which has almost driven heart-religion out of the world; and, Secondly, to warn those who know the religion of the heart, the faith which worketh by love, lest at any time they make void the law through faith, and so fall back into the snare of the devil. *Preface (to the Sermons), Vol. 5, p. 4*

I am a creature of a day, passing through life as an arrow through the air. I am a spirit come from God, and returning to God: Just hovering over the great gulf; until, a few moments hence, I am no more seen: I drop into an unchangeable eternity! I want to know one thing,—the way to heaven; how to land safe on that happy shore. God himself has condescended to teach the way: For this very end he came from heaven. He hath written it down in a book. O give me that book! At any price, give me the book of God! I have it: Here is knowledge enough for me. Let me be *homo unius libri*. (1) Here then I am, far from the busy ways of men. I sit down alone: Only God is here. In his presence I open, I read his book, for this end, to find the way to heaven. Is there a doubt concerning the meaning of what I read? Does anything appear dark or intricate? I lift up my heart to the Father of Lights:— "Lord, is it not thy word, 'If any man lack wisdom, let him ask of God?' Thou 'givest liberally, and upbraidest not.' Thou hast said, 'If any be willing to do thy will, he shall know.' I am willing to do, let me know, thy will." I then search after and consider parallel passages of Scripture, "comparing spiritual things with spiritual." I meditate thereon with all the attention and earnestness of which my mind is capable. If any doubt still remains, I consult those who are experienced in the things of God.... *Preface (to the Sermons), Vol. 5, p. 3*

Consider the Lord's Supper, Secondly, as a mercy from God to man. As God, whose mercy is over all his works, and particularly over the children of men, knew there was but one way for man to be happy like himself; namely, by being like him in holiness; as he knew we could do nothing towards this of ourselves, he has given us certain means of obtaining his help. One of these is the Lord's Supper, which, of his infinite mercy, he hath given us for this very end; that through this means we may be assisted to attain those blessings which he hath prepared for us; that we may obtain holiness on earth, and everlasting glory in heaven. *Sermon 10, The Duty of Constant Communion, Vol. 7, p. 150*

But suppose it were not forbidden how can you, on principles of reason, spend your money in a way which God may possibly forgive, instead of spending it in a manner which he will certainly reward? You will have no reward in heaven for what you lay up; you will, for what you lay out. Every pound you put into the earthly bank is sunk: It brings no interest above. But every pound you give to the poor is put into the bank of heaven. And it will bring glorious interest; yea, and, as such, will be accumulating to all eternity. *Sermon 89, The More Excellent Way, Vol. 7, p. 37*

But allowing that "the friendship of the world is enmity against God," and, consequently, that it is the most excellent way, indeed the only way to heaven, to avoid all intimacy with worldly men; yet who has resolution to walk therein? who even of those that love or fear God? for these only are concerned in the present question. A few I have known who, even in this respect, were lights in a benighted land; who did not and would not either contract or continue any acquaintance with persons of the most refined and improved understanding, and the most engaging tempers, merely because they were of the world. *Sermon 80, On Friendship with the World, Vol. 6, p. 462*

But "without holiness no man shall see the Lord," shall see the face of God in glory. Of consequence, the new birth is absolutely necessary in order to eternal salvation. Men may indeed flatter themselves (so desperately wicked and so deceitful is the heart of man!) that they may live in their sins till they come to the last gasp, and yet afterwards live with God; and thousands do really believe, that they have found a broad way which leadeth not to destruction. "What danger," say they, "can a woman be in that is so *harmless* and so *virtuous*? What fear is there that so honest a man, one of so strict *morality*, should miss of heaven; especially if, over and above all this, they constantly attend on church and sacrament?" One of these will ask with all assurance, "What! shall not I do as well as my neighbours?" Yes, as well as your unholy neighbours; as well as your neighbours that die in their sins! For you will all drop into the pit together; into the nethermost hell! You will all lie together in the lake of fire; "the lake of fire burning with brimstone." Then, at length, you will see (but God grant you may see it before!) the necessity of holiness in order to glory; and, consequently, of the new birth, since none can be holy, except he be born again. *Sermon 45, The New Birth, Vol. 6, p. 72*

Therefore strive ye now, in this your day, to "enter in at the strait gate." And in order thereto, settle it in your heart, and let it be ever uppermost in your thoughts, that if you are in a broad way, you are in the way that leadeth to destruction. If many go with you, as sure as God is true, both they and you are going to hell! If you are walking as the generality of men walk, you are walking to the bottomless pit! Are many wise, many rich, many mighty, or noble, travelling with you in the same way? By this token, without going any farther, you know it does not lead to life. Here is a short, a plain, an infallible rule, before you enter into particulars. In whatever profession you are engaged, you must be singular, or be damned! The way to hell has nothing singular in it; but the way to heaven is singularity all over. If you move but one step towards God, you are not as other men are. But regard not this. It is far better to stand alone, than to fall into the pit. Run, then, with patience the race which is set before thee, though thy companions therein are but few. They will not always be so. Yet a little while, and thou wilt "come to an innumerable company of angels, to the general assembly and Church of the first-born, and to the spirits of just men made perfect." *Sermon 31, Sermon on the Mount — Discourse 11, Vol. 5, p. 412*

And what is it which He is teaching? The Son of God, who came from heaven, is here showing us the way to heaven; to the place which he hath prepared for us; the glory he had before the world began. He is teaching us the true way to life everlasting; the royal way which leads to the kingdom; and the only true way,—for there is none besides; all other paths lead to destruction. From the character of the Speaker, we are well assured that he hath declared the full and perfect will of God. He hath uttered not one tittle too much,—nothing more than he had received of the Father; nor too little,—he hath not shunned to declare the whole counsel of God; much less hath he uttered anything wrong, anything contrary to the will of him that sent him. All his words are true and right concerning all things, and shall stand fast for ever and ever. *Sermon 21, Sermon on the Mount, Discourse 1, Vol. 5, p. 248*

Once more: The Scriptures teach, "This is the love of God," the sure mark thereof, "that we keep his commandments." (1 John v.3.) And our Lord himself saith, "He that keepeth my commandments, he it is that loveth me." (John xiv.21.) Love rejoices to obey; to do, in every point, whatever is acceptable to the beloved. A true lover of God hastens to do his will on earth as it is done in heaven. But is this the character of the presumptuous pretender to the love of God? Nay, but his love gives him a liberty to disobey, to break, not keep the commandments of God. Perhaps, when he was in fear of the wrath of God, he did labour to do his will. But now, looking on himself as "not under the law," he thinks he is no longer obliged to observe it. He is therefore less zealous of good works; less careful to abstain from evil; less watchful over his own heart; less zealous over his tongue. He is less earnest to deny himself, and to take up his cross daily. In a word, the whole form of his life is changed, since he has fancied himself to be at liberty. He is no longer "exercising himself unto godliness;" "wrestling not only with flesh and blood, but with principalities and powers," enduring hardships, "agonizing to enter in at the strait gate." No; he has found an easier way to heaven; a broad, smooth, flowery path; in which he can say to his soul, "Soul, take thy ease; eat, drink, and be merry." It follows, with undeniable evidence, that he has not the true testimony of his own spirit. He cannot be conscious of having those marks which he hath not; that lowliness, meekness, and obedience: Nor yet can the Spirit of the God of truth bear witness to a lie; or testify that he is a child of God, when he is manifestly a child of the devil. *Sermon 10, The Witness of the Spirit, Vol. 5, p. 120*

When he had done preaching, he desired the society to meet; to whom he first gave out an hymn, as before, and then exhorted them to love one another: 1. Because they had one Creator, Preserver, and Father: 2. Because they had all one Redeemer: 3. Because they had all one Sanctifier: 4. Because they were walking in one way of holiness; and, 5. Because they were all going to one heaven. *Journal, Vol. 2, p. 292*

21

Opposition Along the Way

❖— *Scripture Sentence*
Blessed are those who are persecuted for righteousness' sake, for theirs is the kingdom of heaven. *Matthew 5:10*

❖— *Scripture Readings*

Acts 5:12-21
Matthew 13:54-58
*John 15:18-27
1 Corinthians 4:1-13

Matthew 10:16-23
Matthew 10:24-33
Romans 12:14-21

❖— *Silence for Meditation*

❖— *Spiritual Reading*

❖— *Recording Insights and Commitments*

❖— *Prayers of Thanks, Intercession, Petition, and Praise*

❖— *Hymn Portion*
Thou hidden source of calm repose, thou all-sufficient love divine, my help and refuge from my foes, secure I am if thou art mine; and lo! from sin and grief and shame I hide me, Jesus, in thy name. *UMH #153*

❖— *Offering All of Life to God*

❖— *Closing Affirmation*
Finally, be strong in the Lord and in the strength of his power. Put on the whole armor of God, so that you may be able to stand against the wiles of the devil. *Ephesians 6:10-11*

———— Reflections ————

A casual glimpse at the life of John Wesley may lead us to believe that life for him was without opposition. He knew where God was calling him to go, who God was calling him to be, and the rest was simple. In retrospect, we may think that he chose a difficult way of discipleship, but that once the decision was made, and in spite of personal hardship, there was little internal or external opposition.

A deeper gaze at his life and ministry as revealed through his writing and the testimony of those who wrote about him suggests that he faced real opposition from the beginning until the end. Life was not simple or easy. The struggle for faithful discipleship resulted in opposition within his own life and opposition from those who could not agree with the way he had chosen. The search for authentic discipleship led him to go far beyond the common understanding or practice of the Christian faith, and this going beyond the commonly accepted way often led to opposition.

Some opposition arose because of his theology. He stood against a closed system of predestination. He was an ardent witness for God's grace that was active in every life. His conviction that we are justified not by merit but by grace through faith alone raised questions and prompted opposition. His unrelenting commitment to personal and social holiness led him to an unpopular view of piety, riches, and responsibility for the poor. These convictions were rooted in his theology and nurtured by his experience. So opposition grew to his theology and his practice of that theology. Seeking to live out his faith, he was led to what appeared to be a radical response to the call to discipleship. Such a radical response sent shock waves through the Anglican church and the culture and prompted external criticism and opposition.

There was also inner opposition. Wesley's journal reveals that he struggled for faith, questioned his own theology, was perplexed by his own journey toward perfection, and often felt that he had himself missed the mark and failed to practice what he preached.

The opposition he faced through all of life did not result in a gloomy attitude about life or the Christian faith. William Barclay says that a gloomy Christian is a contradiction in terms. I think Wesley would have agreed. He was able to see through the cross of life to the empty tomb.

Opposition then became another gift from God to direct, form, and shape his journey of discipleship.

Any serious attempt to practice a simple but radical discipleship is certain to bring opposition today. We, as Wesley before us and as the saints before him, also know the struggle of internal and external opposition. In a time when division, violence, lust, and greed are the acclaimed way of life, the proclamation of the gospel of Jesus Christ and the attempt to live out that gospel will stir up opposition within and without.

The powers of this world do not want to see their authority and control usurped by another, even if that other is God. To preach a message and practice a life of authentic discipleship will make us uncomfortable and make others anxious and sometimes hostile. We are not above the struggle of what it means to follow Jesus. The complex issues of life do not lend themselves to easy answers. It is not easy to know with certainty the path we are to follow. And often, after careful discernment, the direction we hear is not the way we would have chosen. There is often resistance within us to the way we are convinced God is calling us to travel. It is a strenuous journey of faith that permits us to say with Mary, "Here am I, the servant of the Lord; let it be with me according to your word" (Luke 1:38).

We should not expect instantly to be where Mary was in her witness. Neither should we think that there is something wrong with us because we struggle with internal or external opposition. Self examination and the help of a faithful spiritual guide are ways to test our perceptions with reality.

The good news is that the scriptures, tradition, the experience of the saints, and our own experience tell us that it is possible to face the unknown and even to face opposition without fear and without defeat. To expect a life without struggle is unrealistic. But it is realistic to expect God's help in living an authentic and joyful life as a Christian. To daily declare our love for God and neighbor, to give ourselves as fully as we can to God, and to ask for God's help in living an authentic life of faith is to be prepared to meet any and all opposition. Once we have given all of life to God, we have nothing to lose. We have everything because God has us.

—— *Spiritual Reading* ——

Attacks on the Methodists and other evangelicals were broadly of two kinds: physical and verbal. The physical attacks came mainly in the form of individual and casual assaults and, more spectacularly, as mob violence. The verbal attacks came in many forms and at various levels. They could be a matter of vulgar abuse, satire in prose, verse and drama. To this should be added 'visual' attacks in cartoons and even in pottery. . . . At a more serious and considered level there were attacks by clergy and laity in sermons and pamphlets, which were those most generally answered by Wesley himself. Attacks could also come in the legal forms of episcopal discipline and secular court cases for violations of church order or anti-Dissenting legislation.

Mob violence produced some of the most spectacular and heroic episodes in early Methodist history and was the subject of some dramatic set-pieces in lives of Wesley, as indeed it was in his own *Journal*. Like the verbal attacks, mob attacks have been seen mainly through Methodist eyes and Wesley's responses. . . . It has been natural to assume that attacks on such harmless and indeed virtuous folk were inspired either by people of loose principles offended by the moral demands of the Revival or by rationalistic clergy confronted with a more orthodox creed. Mob violence in particular could easily be seen as mindless hooliganism, sometimes led by clergy and squires in defence of vested interests. *Henry D. Rack, Reasonable Enthusiast, p. 270*

Wesley's honesty about his own situation allows all of us, who have theological doubts or weaknesses in ability, to hope for a new spirit. He faced constant challenges of doubt and self-confidence, writing in his JOURNAL on October 14, 1738: "I cannot find in myself the love of God, or of Christ . . . I have not that joy in the Holy Ghost; no settled, lasting joy. Nor have I such a peace as excludes the possibility either of fear or doubt. When holy men have told me I had no faith . . . I have often doubted whether . . . I had or no. . . ."

Almost a year after Aldersgate, on January 4, 1739, he recorded: "My friends affirm I am mad, because I said I was not a Christian a year ago. I affirm I am not a Christian now. Indeed, what I might have been I know not, had I been faithful to the grace then given, when, expecting nothing less, I received such a sense of forgiveness of my sins as till then I never knew. But that I am not a Christian at this day, ... For a Christian is one who has the fruits of the Spirit of Christ, which ... are love, peace, joy. But these I have not." *Blaine Taylor, John Wesley: A Blueprint for Church Renewal, pp. 82–83*

I do not know that any writer has made any objection against that tract to this day; and for some time: I did not find much opposition upon the head, at least, not from serious persons. But after a time, a cry arose, and, what a little surprised me, among religious men, who affirmed, not that I stated perfection wrong, but that "there is no perfection on earth;" nay, and fell vehemently on my brother and me for affirming the contrary. We scarce expected so rough an attack from these; especially as we were clear on justification by faith, and careful to ascribe the whole of salvation to the mere grace of God. But what most surprised us, was, that we were said to "dishonour Christ," by asserting that he "saveth to the uttermost;" by maintaining he will reign in our hearts alone, and subdue all things to himself. *A Plain Account of Christian Perfection, Vol. 11, p. 374*

Nay, rather, "rejoice and be exceeding glad," when men persecute you for his sake; when they persecute you by reviling you, and by "saying all manner of evil against you falsely:" which they will not fail to mix with every kind of persecution: They must blacken you to excuse themselves: "For so persecuted they the Prophets which were before you!"—those who were most eminently holy in heart and life; yea, and all the righteous which ever have been from the beginning of the world. Rejoice, because by this mark also ye know unto whom ye belong; and "because great is your reward in heaven,"—the reward purchased by the blood of the covenant, and freely bestowed in proportion to your sufferings, as well as to your holiness of heart and life. "Be exceeding glad;" knowing that these "light afflictions, which are but for a moment, work out for you a far more exceeding and eternal weight of glory." *Sermon 23, Sermon on the Mount—Discourse 3, Vol. 5, p. 291*

Yet on Wednesday did I grieve the Spirit of God, not only by not watching unto prayer, but likewise by speaking with sharpness instead of tender love, of one that was not sound in the faith. Immediately God hid his face, and I was troubled; and in this heaviness I continued till the next morning, June 1: When it pleased God, while I was exhorting another, to give comfort to my soul, and (after I had spent some time in prayer) to direct me to those gracious words, "Having therefore boldness to enter into the holiest by the blood of Jesus, let us draw near with a true heart in full assurance of faith. Let us hold fast the profession of our faith without wavering; (for He is faithful that promised;) and let us consider one another to provoke unto love and to good works." *Journal, Vol. 1, p. 105*

But about September, 1739, while my brother and I were absent, certain men crept in among them unawares, greatly troubling and subverting their souls; telling them, they were in a delusion, that they had deceived themselves, and had no true faith at all. "For," said they, "none has any justifying faith, who has ever any doubt or fear, which you know you have; or who has not a clean heart, which you know you have not: Nor will you ever have it, till you leave off using the means of grace; (so called;) till you leave off running to church and sacrament, and praying, and singing, and reading either the Bible, or any other book; for you cannot use these things without trusting in them. Therefore, till you leave them off, you can never have true faith; you can never till then trust in the blood of Christ." *Journal, Vol. 1, p. 81*

I never saw before, no, not at Walsal itself, the hand of God so plainly shown as here. There I had many companions who were willing to die with me: Here, not a friend, but one simple girl, who likewise was hurried away from me in an instant, as soon as ever she came out of Mrs. B.'s door. There I received some blows, lost part of my clothes, and was covered over with dirt: Here, although the hands of perhaps some hundreds of people were lifted up to strike or throw, yet they were one and all stopped in the mid-way; so that not a man touched me with one of his fingers; neither was any thing thrown from first to last; so that I had not even a speck of dirt on my clothes. Who can deny that God heareth the prayer, or that he hath all power in heaven and earth? *Journal, Vol. 1, p. 505*

I do not remember that we met with any person who answered any of these questions in the negative; or who even doubted, whether it were not lawful to apply to this use that time and money which we should else have spent in other diversions. But several we met with who increased our little stock of money for the prisoners and the poor, by subscribing something quarterly to it; so that the more persons we proposed our designs to, the more we were confirmed in the belief of their innocency, and the more determined to pursue them, in spite of the ridicule, which increased fast upon us during the winter. However, in spring I thought it could not be improper to desire farther instructions from those who were wiser and better than ourselves; and, accordingly, (on May 18th, 1731,) I wrote a particular account of all our proceedings to a Clergyman of known wisdom and integrity. After having informed him of all the branches of our design, as clearly and simply as I could, I next acquainted him with the success it had met with, in the following words:—"Almost as soon as we had made our first attempts this way, some of the men of wit in Christ Church entered the lists against us; and, between mirth and anger, made a pretty many reflections upon the Sacramentarians, as they were pleased to call us. Soon after, their allies at Merton changed our title, and did us the honour of styling us, The Holy Club. But most of them being persons of well-known characters, they had not the good fortune to gain any proselytes from the sacrament, till a gentleman, eminent for learning, and well esteemed for piety, joining them, told his nephew, that if he dared to go to the weekly communion any longer, he would immediately turn him out of doors. That argument, indeed, had no success: The young gentleman communicated next week; upon which his uncle, having, again tried to convince him that he was in the wrong way, by shaking him by the throat to no purpose, changed his method, and by mildness prevailed upon him...." *Introductory Letter, Vol. 1, p. 11*

22

The Ministry of All God's People

❖— *Scripture Sentence*
The gifts he gave were that some would be apostles, some prophets, some evangelists, some pastors and teachers, to equip the saints for the work of ministry, for building up the body of Christ. *Ephesians 4:11-12*

❖— *Scripture Readings*

1 Corinthians 1:1-9   1 Thessalonians 1:2-10
*Matthew 12:46-50   Luke 24:44-53
1 Timothy 3:1-13   John 12:20-36
Matthew 7:21-28

❖— *Silence for Meditation*

❖— *Spiritual Reading*

❖— *Recording Insights and Commitments*

❖— *Prayers of Thanks, Intercession, Petition, and Praise*

❖— *Hymn Portion*
He bids us build each other up; and, gathered into one, to our high calling's glorious hope we hand in hand go on. *UMH #554*

❖— *Offering All of Life to God*

❖— *Closing Affirmation*
The general ministry of all Christians in Christ's name is both a gift and a task. The gift is unmerited grace; the task is unstinting service. *The Book of Discipline of The United Methodist Church 1996, Par. 106*

——— Reflections ———

Shared ministry has always been integral to the health, life, and fruitfulness of the church. Jesus quickly enlisted followers and gave them power and authority for ministry. John Wesley went against conventional wisdom in seeking to establish a new equality of ministry among men and women and among preachers and laity. His investment of authority for ministry in laity was astounding and not always understood. While others sought to limit women in their leadership role, he offered an expanded role for women in the life and mission of the church.

Wesley knew how important it was that each part of the body of Christ fulfill its responsibility. He could see that men and women were equally gifted for ministry and should be given liberty to exercise their gifts. He noted that where opportunity for ministry was given, fruitfulness was the result. He also knew that clergy and laity were necessary to the effectiveness and faithfulness of the church. Each had a distinctive role to play and only when those distinctive roles were fulfilled could there be harmony, unity, faithfulness, and effectiveness.

In Wesley's world everything was carefully structured. This concern for organization and structure was seen in every part of his life, from his practice of spiritual disciplines, his keeping of a journal, his relentless schedule, and his careful assignment of responsibility to all who sought to follow Christ as Methodists. His desire for full engagement of all in the mission of the church led him to careful organization and delegation of responsibilities. Every follower of Jesus Christ had a mission to fulfill and organization was the way to accomplish that task.

This delegation of responsibilities resulted in an effective organization and contributed to the rapid growth and expansion of the Methodist movement. Thomas Langford, in his book *Practical Divinity*, notes Wesley's inclusive reach to enlist all who would follow Jesus in the ministry of the Church. "Priest, cobbler, schoolmaster, baker, printer, stonemason, all were invited to participate in this shared ministry of loving God and neighbor with all heart, mind, soul and strength" (p. 17).

The ministry of all Christians as a concept is more acceptable today and yet its achievement is often elusive. Clergy and laity often see this concept as an issue of power. When they do, the struggle for supremacy or power renders ministry ineffective and is usually destructive to all involved. This is not a new problem. Jesus faced it with disciples who sought special "power" positions and Wesley faced it when lay and clergy were in conflict over "control" issues. We face it today in similar ways.

We believe that Jesus included all in the encircling embrace of God and rejected discrimination as a means of achieving status, position, or power. His ministry was to all persons, for all persons, and with all persons. A faithful church will reflect this welcoming and involving of all in a shared ministry of proclaiming and practicing the gospel. While this concept sounds simple and easy, it is not.

For centuries clergy and laity have "staked out" their territory as a means of exerting power and control in the church. This territory once claimed for self or group is not easily surrendered, even to God!

Wesley spoke often of the deadness of preachers and laity. Where preachers were dead, the mission of the church was held back and where laity were dead the mission of the Church was rendered ineffective. And yet, he never lost hope that the "dead bones" could take on life once again. And often, his admonishment, leading, and direction became the channel through which the power of the Holy Spirit awakened new life in clergy and laity alike. And when this new life was awakened in clergy and laity, remarkable effectiveness was almost certain to follow.

What would it take to fully invest all of the gifts for ministry that are latent in every person, every congregation, and every denomination? Perhaps we could all agree that the place of beginning is an unqualified giving of each of our lives to God. Life totally given to God is available for direction and investment anywhere. Life totally given to God is available to be sent and employed at any time, any place, any position, and in any mission that God chooses. To offer life to God fully and without reservation is not an easy commitment to make. And when made it is not achieved once and for all. Rather, the "going on to perfection" is a lifelong journey. The good news is that we do not make that journey alone. Shared ministry is a natural consequence of following Jesus. May it be one of the marks that distinguishes you and your congregation.

——— *Spiritual Reading* ———

When the people joined together, simply to help each other to heaven, increased by hundreds and thousands, still they had no more thought of leaving the Church than of leaving the kingdom. Nay, I continually and earnestly cautioned them against it; reminding them that we were a part of the Church of England, whom God had raised up, not only to save our own souls, but to enliven our neighbours, those of the Church in particular. *Farther Thoughts on Separation from the Church, Vol. 13, p. 272*

O contain yourselves within your own bounds; be content with preaching the gospel; "do the work of Evangelists;" proclaim to all the world the lovingkindness of God our Savior; declare to all, "The kingdom of heaven is at hand: Repent ye, and believe the gospel!" I earnestly advise you, abide in your place; keep your own station. Ye were, fifty years ago, those of you that were then Methodist Preachers, *extraordinary messengers* of God, not going in your own will, but *thrust out*, not to supersede but to "provoke to jealousy," the ordinary messengers. In God's name, stop there! Both by your preaching and example provoke them to love and to good works. Ye are a new phenomenon in the earth,—a body of people who, being of no sect or party, are friends to all parties, and endeavour to forward all in heart-religion, in the knowledge and love of God and man. Ye yourselves were at first called in the Church of England; and though ye have and will have a thousand temptations to leave it, and set up for yourselves, regard them not; be Church-of-England men still; do not cast away the peculiar glory which God hath put upon you, and frustrate the design of Providence, the very end for which God raised you up. *Sermon 115, The Ministerial Office, Vol. 7, p. 280*

We returned to London. Monday, 11. I went on to Colchester, and still found matter of humiliation. The society was lessened, and cold enough; preaching again was discontinued, and the spirit of Methodism quite gone, both from the Preachers and the people. Yet we had a wonderful congregation in the evening, rich and poor, Clergy and laity. So we had likewise on Tuesday evening. So that I trust God will at length build up the waste places. *Journal, Vol. 4, p. 497*

The congregation at five filled the House almost as well as it was filled in the evening. Finding a remarkable deadness, I inquired what were the reasons of it; and found, 1. There had been, for several months, a deep misunderstanding between the Preachers and the chief of the society. Hence, on the one hand, the Preachers had little life or spirit to preach; and, on the other, the congregation dwindled away. 2. Many had left off meeting their bands, and many others seldom met their classes. 3. Prayer-meetings were entirely given up. What wonder if all the people were grown dead as stones? *Journal, Vol. 4, p. 375*

About twelve I preached at Lane-End. It being too cold to stand abroad, the greater part of the earnest congregation squeezed into the preaching-house. Here we entered into the country which seems to be all on fire,—that which borders on Burslem on every side: Preachers and people provoking one another to love and good works, in such a manner as was never seen before. In the evening I preached at Burslem. Observing the people flocking together, I began half an hour before the appointed time. But, notwithstanding this, the House would not contain one half of the congregation: So, while I was preaching in the House to all that could get in, John Broadbent preached in a yard to the rest. The love-feast followed; but such a one as I have not known for many years. While the two or three first spoke, the power of God so fell upon all that were present, some praying, and others giving thanks, that their voices could scarce be heard: And two or three were speaking at a time, till I gently advised them to speak one at a time; and they did so, with amazing energy. *Journal, Vol. 4, p. 365*

In the evening I talked largely with the Preachers, and showed them the hurt it did both to them and the people, for any one Preacher to stay six or eight weeks together in one place. Neither can he find matter for preaching every morning and evening, nor will the people come to hear him. Hence he grows cold by lying in bed, and so do the people. Whereas, if he never stays more than a fortnight together in one place, he may find matter enough, and the people will gladly hear him. They immediately drew up such a plan for this Circuit, which they determined to pursue. *Journal, Vol. 4, p. 273*

I made an odd observation here, which I recommend to all our Preachers. The people of Canterbury have been so often reproved, (and frequently without a cause,) for being dead and cold, that it has utterly discouraged them, and made them cold as stones. How delicate a thing is it to reprove! To do it well, requires more than human wisdom. *Journal, Vol. 3, p. 348*

I rode on to Pembroke, and, this and the next evening, preached in the main street, to far more than the House could have contained. . . . Upon inquiry, I found the work of God in Pembrokeshire had been exceedingly hindered, chiefly by Mr. Davies's Preachers, who had continually inveighed against ours, and thereby frightened abundance of people from hearing, or coming near them. This had sometimes provoked them to retort, which always made a bad matter worse. The advice, therefore, which I gave them was, 1. Let all the people sacredly abstain from backbiting, tale-bearing, evil-speaking: 2. Let all our Preachers abstain from returning railing for railing, either in public or in private; as well as from disputing: 3. Let them never preach controversy, but plain, practical, and experimental religion. *Journal, Vol. 3, p. 296*

We returned to Epworth, to a poor, dead, senseless people: At which I did not wonder, when I was informed, 1. That some of our Preachers there had diligently gleaned up and retailed all the evil they could hear of me: 2. That some of them had quite laid aside our hymns, as well as the doctrine they formerly preached: 3. That one of them had frequently spoke against our Rules, and the others quite neglected them. Nothing, therefore, but the mighty power of God could have kept the people so well as they were. *Journal, Vol. 2, p. 230*

The ministry of all Christians consists of service for the mission of God in the world. The mission of God is best expressed in the prayer that Jesus taught his first disciples: Thy kingdom come; thy will be done, on earth as in heaven.

All Christians, therefore, are to live in active expectancy: faithful in service of God and their neighbor; faithful in waiting for the fulfillment of God's universal love, justice, and peace on earth as in heaven.

Pending this time of fulfillment, the ministry of all Christians is shaped by the teachings of Jesus. The handing on of these teachings is entrusted to leaders who are gifted and called by God to appointed offices in the church: some apostles, some prophets, some evangelists, some pastors and teachers, to equip the saints for the work of ministry, for building up the body of Christ (Ephesians 4:11-12). For these persons to lead the church effectively, they must embody the teachings of Jesus in servant ministries and servant leadership. Through these ministries and leadership, congregations of the church are faithfully engaged in the forming of Christian disciples and vitally involved in the mission of God in the world....

Servant Ministry

Christian Discipleship—The ministry of all Christians consists of privilege and obligation. The privilege is a relationship with God that is deeply spiritual. The obligation is to respond to God's call to holy living in the world. In the United Methodist tradition these two dimensions of Christian discipleship are wholly interdependent.

Our Relationship with God: Privilege—Christians experience growth and transition in their spiritual life just as in their physical and emotional lives. While this growth is always a work of grace, it does not occur uniformly. Spiritual growth in Christ is a dynamic process marked by awakening, birth, growth, and maturation. This process requires careful and intentional nurture for the disciple to reach perfection in the Christian life. There are stages of spiritual growth and transition: Christian beginnings; Christian birth; Christian growth; and Christian maturity. These require careful and intentional nurture for the disciple to come to maturity in the Christian life and to engage fully in the ministry of all Christians.

Our Relationship with Christ in the World: Obligation—The ministry of all Christians in the United Methodist tradition has always been energized by deep religious experience, with emphasis on how ministry relates to our obligation to Jesus Christ. *The Book of Discipline of The United Methodist Church 1996, pp. 110–11 (Par. 110–14)*

23

Sanctifying Grace

❖— *Scripture Sentence*
May the God of peace himself sanctify you entirely.
1 Thessalonians 5:23

❖— *Scripture Readings*

1 Corinthians 1:26-31   Hebrews 10:11-18
1 Thessalonians 4:1-8   *John 17:11-19
Ezekiel 20:8-13   Acts 26:12-18
Hebrews 10:1-10

❖— *Silence for Meditation*

❖— *Spiritual Reading*

❖— *Recording Insights and Commitments*

❖— *Prayers of Thanks, Intercession, Petition, and Praise*

❖— *Hymn Portion*
Only let us persevere till we see our Lord appear,
never from the Rock remove, saved by faith which
works by love. *UMH #385*

❖— *Offering All of Life to God*

❖— *Closing Affirmation*
But you were washed, you were sanctified, you were
justified in the name of the Lord Jesus Christ and in
the Spirit of our God. *1 Corinthians 6:11*

——— *Reflections* ———

Can we be good on our own? Can we do good on our own? Can we live a life of goodness, holiness on our own? The thriving business of self-help books and programs suggests that we can. Some believe that if we are wise enough, tough enough, persistent enough, and try just a little harder we can do it all on our own. John Wesley believed that it was impossible without the help of God. Salvation and sanctification are always out of reach without the action of God.

Wesley was not naive about the reality and power of sin. He was a careful observer of life in the church and in the world. He was also one who practiced careful self-examination. From observation and personal experience, he was convinced that sin was never far from anyone. Not only was sin near to us, it was also powerful, so powerful that humans were not strong enough to overcome its power and contagion. Sin, evil, our shadow side, whatever we call it, was a very real problem.

The good news he preached was that there is remedy for this problem. The problem can be solved; we can receive forgiveness through God's justifying grace. We can find assurance that sins are forgiven. The sins of the past, no matter how abhorrent, can be forgiven, blotted out and removed. We do not need to carry the burden of unforgiven sin. The remedy is forgiveness through God's justifying grace. This is something God does for us since we are powerless to do it for ourselves. Through faith we may claim this justifying grace and its fruit for our own lives. There is no need for anyone to end the day, or to end life, burdened by sin. Our salvation is secured for us and offered to us in the life, death, and resurrection of Jesus Christ. Only our faith is required to claim this gift for ourselves.

Wesley also preached the good news that God not only does something for us (that is, saves us in this world and the next), but God also does something within us. He believed and taught that God desires that we live lives of holiness. Because of the power of sin, the only possible road to this reality is the sanctifying grace of God at work within us. He taught that by cooperating with this sanctifying grace within we could journey on the road to perfection. Salvation was not only for the world to come but was to be enjoyed and lived out in the world of everyday life. To do so requires God's intervention and transformation within.

It is God's sanctifying grace at work within us that leads to transformation. It is the inner life that must be transformed if the outer life is to be changed. The desire for this transformation, as the transformation itself, is God at work within us. Sanctifying grace does not relieve us of our responsibility to love God and neighbor. It does assure us that by God's grace we can practice what scripture teaches as the greatest commandments of all.

Wesley believed that the new birth was more than forgiveness and assurance. It involved "going on to perfection," a journey that all were challenged to pursue and a journey that none could make on their own. The life of holiness was the goal for everyone and sanctifying grace provided the desire and capacity to pursue it daily.

No Christian should live with the weight of unforgiven sin and unresolved guilt. The assurance that we are forgiven, that we can begin again with a new page of life upon which to write our story, is the gift of God's justifying grace for all. But this is not the end of our relationship with God, the end of faith, or the end of our journey toward righteousness. Rather, it is the beginning of a quest for a life of goodness and holiness.

Our age is noted for its turbulence, rapid and radical change. This setting makes living a life of holiness even more difficult. When we desire salvation, forgiveness for our sins, we respond to the Holy Spirit awakening us to our need. When we yearn for a heart of love for God and neighbor, we respond to the Holy Spirit awakening us to our need of a pure heart and a holy life. This awakening is illustration of God's grace within.

In our better moments all of us want to walk with Jesus Christ in faithful companionship. We know from experience that it is not easy to do in our complex and broken world. The temptations and opportunities to be less than like Christ surround us daily. However the grace to be more than we are is even closer. It is God's work of transformation within, and it is offered to everyone. Sanctifying grace is already at work within us. Our challenge is to cooperate with openness to God and by receiving the gift of sanctifying grace. It is this grace, coupled with our disciplined life, that leads to a life of peace, assurance, faithfulness, and usefulness. It is this grace that leads us on the journey toward Christian perfection.

───── *Spiritual Reading* ─────

From the time of our being born again, the gradual work of sanctification takes place. We are enabled "by the Spirit" to "mortify the deeds of the body," of our evil nature; and as we are more and more dead to sin, we are more and more alive to God. We go on from grace to grace, while we are careful to "abstain from all appearance of evil," and are "zealous of good works," as we have opportunity, doing good to all men; while we walk in all His ordinances blameless, therein worshiping Him in spirit and in truth; while we take up our cross, and deny ourselves every pleasure that does not lead us to God. S*ermon 43, The Scripture Way of Salvation, Vol. 6, p. 46*

They speak of sanctification (or holiness) as if it were an outward thing; as if it consisted chiefly, if not wholly, in those two points, 1. The doing no harm; 2. The doing good, (as it is called,) that is, the using the means of grace, and helping our neighbour. I believe it to be an inward thing, namely, the life of God in the soul of man; a participation of the divine nature; the mind that was in Christ; or, the renewal of our heart, after the image of Him that created us. *Journal, Vol. 1, p. 225*

I was desired to go to Bath; where I offered to about a thousand souls the free grace of God to "heal their backsliding;" and in the morning to (I believe) more than two thousand. I preached to about the same number at Baptist-Mills in the afternoon, on, "Christ, made of God unto us, wisdom, and righteousness, and sanctification, and redemption." *Journal, Vol. 1, p. 186*

Indeed the leading of the Spirit is different in different souls. His more usual method, I believe, is, to give, in one and the same moment, the forgiveness of sins, and a full assurance of that forgiveness. Yet in many He works as He did in me: Giving first the remission of sins, and, after some weeks or months or years, the full assurance of it. *Journal, Vol. 1, p. 127*

After my return home, I was much buffeted with temptations; but cried out, and they fled away. They returned again and again. I as often lifted up my eyes, and He "sent me help from his holy place." And herein I found the difference between this and my former state chiefly consisted. I was striving, yea, fighting with all my might under the law, as well as under grace. But then I was sometimes, if not often, conquered; now, I was always conqueror. *Journal, Vol. 1, pp. 103–4*

Several of these, after being thoroughly sensible of their fall, and deeply ashamed before God, have been again filled with his love, and not only perfected therein, but stablished, strengthened, and settled. They have received the blessing they had before with abundant increase. Nay, it is remarkable, that many who had fallen either from justifying or from sanctifying grace, and so deeply fallen that they could hardly be ranked among the servants of God, have been restored, (but seldom till they had been shaken, as it were, over the mouth of hell,) and that very frequently in an instant, to all that they had lost. They have, at once, recovered both a consciousness of his favour, and the experience of the pure love of God. In one moment they received anew both remission of sins, and a lot among them that were sanctified. *Sermon 86, A Call to Backsliders, Vol. 6, p. 526*

The more I converse with the believers in Cornwall, the more I am convinced that they have sustained great loss for want of hearing the doctrine of Christian Perfection clearly and strongly enforced. I see, wherever this is not done, the believers grow dead and cold. Nor can this be prevented, but by keeping up in them an hourly expectation of being perfected in love. I say an hourly expectation; for to expect it at death, or some time hence, is much the same as not expecting it at all. *Journal, Vol. 3, p. 113*

It is certain, God does at some times, without any cause, known to us, shower down his grace in an extraordinary manner. And he does, in some instances, delay to give either justifying or sanctifying grace, for reasons which are not discovered to us. These are some of those secrets of his government, which it hath pleased him to reserve in his own breast. I hope you and your wife keep all you have, and gasp for more. *Letters to Mr. Merryweather, of Yarm, Vol. 12, p. 271*

In universal obedience; in keeping all the commandments; in denying ourselves, and taking up our cross daily. These are the general means which God hath ordained for our receiving his sanctifying grace. The particular are, — prayer, searching the Scripture, communicating, and fasting. *Some Late Conversations, Vol. 8, p. 286*

There is, likewise, great variety in the manner and time of God's bestowing his sanctifying grace, whereby he enables his children to give him their whole heart, which we can in no wise account for. We know not why he bestows this on some, even before they ask for it; (some unquestionable instances of which we have seen;) on some, after they had sought it but a few days: And yet permits other believers to wait for it, perhaps twenty, thirty, or forty years; nay, and others, till a few hours, or even minutes, before their spirits return to him. For the various circumstances also which attend the fulfilling of that great promise, "I will circumcise thy heart, to love the Lord thy God with all thy heart and with all thy soul." God undoubtedly has reasons; but those reasons are generally hid from the children of men. Once more: Some of those who are enabled to love God with all their heart and with all their soul retain the same blessing, without any interruption, till they are carried to Abraham's bosom; others do not retain it, although they are not conscious of having grieved the Holy Spirit of God. This also we do not understand: We do not herein "know the mind of the Spirit." *Sermon 69, The Imperfection of Human Knowledge, Vol. 6, p. 349*

By "means of grace" I understand outward signs, words, or actions, ordained of God, and appointed for this end, to be the ordinary channels whereby he might convey to men, preventing, justifying, or sanctifying grace. *Sermon 16, The Means of Grace, Vol. 5, p. 187*

From at least 1725 until the end of his days, Wesley was committed to the realization of holiness of life. Despite all vicissitudes of formulation and expression, this was the aim of his life, the organizing center of his thought, the spring of all action, his one abiding project. This meant becoming a creature worthy of the Creator, a finite representative and image of the divine subject.

Such a correspondence to the divine life meant a rupture with the world, a transformation of life that separated the new from the old, the spirit from the flesh, the life of faith from the world. The possibility of such a project was based on the divine self-revelation that provided a paradigm and clear instructions for the actualization of this holiness.

The first Methodists (Wesley, his brother Charles, and a few of their friends at Oxford) sought to realize this project. From the very first it entailed a new economic practice, a dedication of all resources to the poor on the basis of the instructions of the Gospels. Some of the other aspects of the practice of the first Methodists were later modified. The adherence to the rubrics of the Church, for example, was later relaxed. But the practice of a new economics, consciously opposed to the economics of "the world," remained despite all changes in interpretation and explanation. . . .

Grace does not, then, provide a dispensation from holiness but serves as the capacitation *for* holiness. In one sense nothing has changed. The insistence upon holiness and the necessity of following the divine instructions to the letter do not vary a hair. In another sense everything is changed in that the basis of this correspondence to the divine is an inward appropriation made possible by grace.

But if grace is the basis of this transformation, then consequences for the *manner* of realizing holiness follow. It is no longer necessary to retire from the world to be holy. Grace is available not just to an elite but to all. Therefore, even those who had before been utterly given over to sin could be utterly renewed by grace. The cloister of Oxford could be exchanged for the fields, the streets, the marketplace, even the gallows. Anyone could become holy in life through the operation of grace.

Thus the holiness project is unleashed upon the world. All people everywhere, and not only contemplative scholars or mystics, were called to correspond to the divine nature, and the grace that would make such a correspondence actual was freely offered to all.

But note that *this* grace is the grace that makes us really and effectively holy. The good news is that we can become holy, not that we have been made exempt from holiness. But holiness is transformed from an elitist to a populist project by the power of grace. *Theodore W. Jennings, Jr. Good News to the Poor, pp. 140–41*

24

The Way Methodists Live

❖— *Scripture Sentence*

He has told you, O mortal, what is good; and what does the Lord require of you but to do justice, and to love kindness, and to walk humbly with your God? *Micah 6:8*

❖— *Scripture Readings*

Luke 12:22-34	James 1:2-18
Acts 11:19-30	*1 John 3:11-24
Matthew 26:69-75	1 Peter 5:1-11
1 Timothy 6:11-16	

❖— *Silence for Meditation*

❖— *Spiritual Reading*

❖— *Recording Insights and Commitments*

❖— *Prayers of Thanks, Intercession, Petition, and Praise*

❖— *Hymn Portion*

Give me the faith which can remove and sink the mountain to a plain; give me the childlike praying love, which longs to build thy house again; thy love, let it my heart o'erpower and all my simple soul devour. *UMH #650*

❖— *Offering All of Life to God*

❖— *Closing Affirmation*

Whoever serves me must follow me, and where I am, there will my servant be also. Whoever serves me, the Father will honor. *John 12:26*

——— Reflections ———

There was a time when Methodists could be recognized very easily. To refer to the history of the Methodist movement in Great Britain and the United States is to discover that Methodists were never easy to hide! Like their father in the faith, Methodists were interested in such simple things as saving faith, the practical ways to keep that faith alive, and a living out of that faith in every aspect of daily life, both private and public.

The conviction ran deep that because of personal commitment and the power of God at work in a person's life, Christians were to be different. Their goals and priorities were not determined by the culture, or even the church, but by a daily companionship with Jesus Christ. The love of God and neighbor led them to stand against all that was destructive of humankind. The consistent stand against injustice and the untiring efforts to create laws and institutions that brought healing, help, and hope to all people set them apart, often to their peril and pain.

No one could follow Jesus Christ and not be identified, and since Methodists were to follow only Christ they were easily recognized. This recognition brought respect as well as derision. But neither counted for anything. The only thing that mattered was faithfulness to God.

Methodist life was marked by a deep and authentic personal piety that led to a broad and uncompromising social involvement. Methodists were known for their prayers and for their commitment to the poor and disenfranchised. This commitment resulted in persistent efforts to build houses of prayer and worship as well as consistent efforts to visit the prisons, build schools and hospitals, and work for laws which moved toward a just and peaceful social order. Not everyone agreed with or applauded the way early Methodists lived, but it did not require many at any one place to make a difference. Because they took their relationship to Jesus Christ with utmost seriousness, their life of prayer and witness was readily identified and often very contagious as many wanted what Methodists appeared to have. Among these Methodist gifts were a certain knowledge of their own salvation, an at-homeness in this world and confidence in the next, a living companionship with a living Christ, and access to the power of God that could and did transform the most broken and hopeless persons into productive, joyful, and faithful disciples. Such was the power of God at work in the way Methodists lived. Methodists believed that they were to be the leaven that God could use to transform the church and the world.

The effort of the world to press all people into its mold is well known in our own culture and community. We hesitate to stand out, especially on faith or social issues. We are often timid in declaring our love for and faith in God and our love for and commitment to neighbor. It is easier to go along with popular opinion than to declare our own opinion that has grown out of deep, earnest, searching prayer. Jesus reminds us that there is cost in following him with unqualified obedience. He also reminds us that there is reward. The reward for this kind of faithfulness is life abundant, life lived to the maximum joy and meaning, life that is rich and full in this world and blessed and eternal in the world to come. Early Methodists were able to claim this promise, and as they did, remarkable transformations took place in their lives and in the society around them. From the beginning, Methodists felt called to live out their faith in practical ways—ways that brought healing and wholeness to individuals and to the human family.

In an age of unprecedented brokenness in the life of the individual and growing fractures in the human family, the practice of the Methodist way of Christian living holds great promise for a more faithful personal life and a more just and peaceful world. Could such a practical, simple and yet radical Christianity flourish in our complex, changing, and confusing world? Only if it is tried!

So, whoever you are reading these pages, I invite you to begin anew to live a life of unqualified commitment to Jesus Christ where you are. Be bold enough to ask God to transform your own life and invest your life as leaven to transform the world where you are. Begin every day in seeking God's direction and companionship, and end every day in offering anew all you have done and all that you are to the One who gives you life. Companionship with the living Christ is the Methodist way of living that God has honored with fruitfulness in the past. May it happen again in our time.

——— *Spiritual Reading* ———

I say, those who are called Methodists; for, let it be well observed, that this is not a name which they take upon themselves, but one fixed on them by way of reproach, without their approbation or consent. It was first given to three or four young men at Oxford, by a Student of Christ's Church; either in allusion to the ancient sect of Physicians, (so called from their teaching that almost all diseases might be cured by a specific method of diet and exercise,) or from their observing a more regular method of study and behaviour than was usual with those of their age and station. *(Preface to "The Character of a Methodist.") A Letter to the Lord Bishop of Gloucester, Vol. 9, p. 130*

Whoever agrees with us in that account of practical religion, given in "The Character of a Methodist," I regard not what his other opinions are; the same is my brother, and sister, and mother. I am more assured that love is of God, than that any opinion whatsoever is so. Herein may we increase more and more. *Letter to the Rev. James Erskine, Vol. 13, p. 162*

But though I aver this, am I "quite indifferent as to any man's opinion in religion?" Far, very far from it; as I have declared again and again in the very sermon under consideration, in the "Character of a Methodist," in the "Plain Account," and twenty tracts besides. Neither do I "conceal my sentiments." Few men less. I have written severally, and printed, against Deists, Papists, Mystics, Quakers, Anabaptists, Presbyterians, Calvinists, and Antinomians. An odd way of ingratiating myself with them, to strike at the apple of their eye! Nevertheless, in all things indifferent, (but not at the expense of truth,) I rejoice to "please all men for their good edification;" if haply I may "gain more proselytes" to genuine, scriptural Christianity; if I may prevail upon the more to love God and their neighbour, and to walk as Christ walked. *Second Letter to the Rev. Mr. Clark, Vol. 13, p. 214*

You conclude your letter with a very just observation; — "The civil and religious rights of mankind have seldom been promoted by the assemblies of Ecclesiastics of any denomination:

And they never will be, unless they are composed of men devoted to God, and dead to all the allurements of ease, and avarice, and ambition." This is undoubtedly true; and this, we humbly hope, is the real character of most (at least) of those persons that meet in our assemblies. We hope, likewise, that "their consultations will always be moderated by some wise and truly religious man;" otherwise, that God will sweep away the very name of Methodist from the earth. *Answer to Objections Against "The Arminian Magazine," Vol. 14, p. 365*

Mr. Garden (to whom I must ever acknowledge myself indebted for many kind and generous offices) desiring me to preach, I did so, on these words of the Epistle of the day: "Whatsoever is born of God, overcometh the world." To that plain account of the Christian state which these words naturally led me to give, a man of education and character seriously objected, (what is indeed a great truth,) "Why, if this be Christianity, a Christian must have more courage than Alexander the Great." *Journal, Vol. 1, p. 47*

The occasion of his late attack is this: — Five or six and thirty years ago, I much admired the character of a perfect Christian drawn by Clemens Alexandrinus. Five or six and twenty years ago, a thought came into my mind, of drawing such a character myself, only in a more scriptural manner, and mostly in the very words of Scripture: This I entitled, "The Character of a Methodist," believing that curiosity would incite more persons to read it, and also that some prejudice might thereby be removed from candid men. But that none might imagine I intended a panegyric either on myself or my friends, I guarded against this in the very title-page, saying, both in the name of myself and them, "Not as though I had already attained, either were already perfect." To the same effect I speak in the conclusion, "These are the principles and practices of our sect; these are the marks of a true Methodist;" *i.e.,* a true Christian, as I immediately after explain myself: "By these alone do those who are in derision so called desire to be distinguished from other men." (p. 11.) "By these marks do we *labour* to distinguish ourselves from those whose minds or lives are not according to the Gospel of Christ." (p. 12.) *Journal, Vol. 3, p. 273*

Here then we see in the clearest, strongest light, what is real religion: A restoration of man by Him that bruises the serpent's head, to all that the old serpent deprived him of; a restoration, not only to the favour but likewise to the image of God, implying not barely deliverance from sin, but the being filled with the fulness of God. It is plain, if we attend to the preceding considerations, that nothing short of this is Christian religion. Every thing else, whether negative or external, is utterly wide of the mark. But what paradox is this! How little is it understood in the Christian world; yea, in this enlightened age, wherein it is taken for granted, the world is wiser than ever it was from the beginning! Among all our discoveries, who has discovered this? How few either among the learned or unlearned! And yet, if we believe the Bible, who can deny it? Who can doubt of it? It runs through the Bible from the beginning to the end, in one connected chain; and the agreement of every part of it, with every other, is, properly, the analogy of faith. Beware of taking any thing else, or any thing less than this, for religion! Not *any thing else*: Do not imagine an outward form, a round of duties, both in public and private, is religion! Do not suppose that honesty, justice, and whatever is called *morality*, (though excellent in its place,) is religion! And least of all dream that orthodoxy, right opinion, (vulgarly called *faith*,) is religion. Of all religious dreams, this is the vainest; which takes hay and stubble for gold tried in the fire! *Sermon 62, The End of Christ's Coming, Vol. 6, p. 276*

There is only one condition previously required of those who desire admission into these societies: "a desire to flee from the wrath to come, and to be saved from their sins." But wherever this is really fixed in the soul it will be shown by its fruits.

It is therefore expected of all who continue therein that they should continue to evidence their desire of salvation,

First: By doing no harm, by avoiding evil of every kind, especially that which is most generally practiced, such as:

The taking of the name of God in vain.

The profaning the day of the Lord, either by doing ordinary work therein or by buying or selling.

Drunkenness: buying or selling spirituous liquors, or drinking them, unless in cases of extreme necessity.

Slaveholding; buying or selling slaves.

Fighting, quarreling, brawling, brother going to law with brother; returning evil for evil, or railing for railing; the using many words in buying or selling.

The buying or selling goods that have not paid the duty.

The giving or taking things on usury—i.e., unlawful interest.

Uncharitable or unprofitable conversation; particularly speaking evil of magistrates or of ministers.

Doing to others as we would not they should do unto us.

Doing what we know is not for the glory of God, as:

The putting on of gold and costly apparel.

The taking such diversions as cannot be used in the name of the Lord Jesus.

The singing those songs, or reading those books, which do not tend to the knowledge or love of God.

Softness and needless self-indulgence.

Laying up treasure upon earth.

Borrowing without a probability of paying; or taking up goods without a probability of paying for them.

It is expected of all who continue in these societies that they should continue to evidence their desire of salvation,

Secondly: By doing good; by being in every kind merciful after their power; as they have opportunity, doing good of every possible sort, and, as far as possible, to all men:

To their bodies, of the ability which God giveth, by giving food to the hungry, by clothing the naked, by visiting or helping them that are sick or in prison.

To their souls, by instructing, reproving, or exhorting all we have any intercourse with; trampling under foot that enthusiastic doctrine that "we are not to do good unless our *hearts be free to it.*"

By doing good, especially to them that are of the household of faith or groaning so to be; employing them preferably to others; buying one of another, helping each other in business, and so much the more because the world will love its own and them only.

By all possible diligence and frugality, that the gospel be not blamed.

By running with patience the race which is set before them, denying themselves, and taking up their cross daily; submitting to bear the reproach of Christ, to be as the filth and offscouring of the world; and looking that men should say all manner of evil of them *falsely*, for the Lord's sake.

It is expected of all who desire to continue in these societies that they should continue to evidence their desire of salvation,

Thirdly: By attending upon all the ordinances of God; such are:

The public worship of God.

The ministry of the Word, either read or expounded.

The Supper of the Lord.

Family and private prayer

Searching the Scriptures.

Fasting or abstinence.

These are the General Rules of our societies; all of which we are taught of God to observe, even in his written Word, which is the only rule, and the sufficient rule, both of our faith and practice. And all these we know his Spirit writes on truly awakened hearts. If there be any among us who observe them not, who habitually break any of them, let it be known unto them who watch over that soul as they who must give an account. We will admonish him of the error of his ways. We will bear with him for a season. But then, if he repent not, he hath no more place among us. We have delivered our own souls. *The Book of Discipline of The United Methodist Church 1996, pp. 70–72 (Par. 62)*

25
God's Love and Ours

❖— *Scripture Sentence*
We love because he first loved us. *1 John 4:19*

❖— *Scripture Readings*

*1 John 3:1-11   John 15:12-17
Matthew 5:43-44   Micah 6:6-8
Matthew 22:34-40   1 John 4:7-12
John 13:31-35

❖— *Silence for Meditation*

❖— *Spiritual Reading*

❖— *Recording Insights and Commitments*

❖— *Prayers of Thanks, Intercession, Petition, and Praise*

❖— *Hymn Portion*
Touched by the lodestone of thy love, let all our hearts agree, and ever toward each other move, and ever move toward thee. *UMH #561*

❖— *Offering All of Life to God*

❖— *Closing Affirmation*
Whoever loves a brother or sister lives in the light, and in such a person there is no cause for stumbling. *1 John 2:10*

—— Reflections ——

The essential nature of the Christian faith and life is love. All else revolves around this vital center, God's love for us, and our awakened love for God and neighbor. And this love is most profoundly, clearly, and simply revealed in the life, death, and resurrection of Jesus Christ. John Wesley's journal, letters, sermons, and biblical commentary all reflect this center for his thought and faith. It provided the energy for the early Methodist movement and still guides the faith and witness of the worldwide Wesleyan movement.

We do love God because God first loved us. Our love is always in response to what God has done and is doing in our lives. Wesley was convinced that we could never love God or neighbor unless God had first loved us. Christians believe it is God in Christ who loves us and seeks and awakens our love in return. It is God who inspires and enables us to love our neighbor. Wesley believed that on our own we are incapable of loving God or neighbor. This is humankind's greatest dilemma. And yet, our inheritance as children of God cannot be claimed until our awakened love responds to God's seeking love.

Charles Wesley captured this central theme of Wesleyan theology in his hymn, "Love Divine, All Loves Excelling." Notice the breadth and depth of thought and feeling in these few lines.

> Love divine, all loves excelling, joy of heaven, to earth come down; fix in us thy humble dwelling, all thy faithful mercies crown! Jesus, thou art all compassion, pure, unbounded love thou art; visit us with thy salvation; enter every trembling heart.

It was this divine love, pure and unbounded, that brought to John Wesley assurance of his own salvation and energized him to share this good news with the world. It was clear to Wesley that our lives, our faith, our salvation, our spiritual journey are all rooted in this unbounded and unconditional love of God.

Having experienced this unearned, undeserved, and unlimited love, it is not surprising that there was awakened in Wesley's heart a burning fire of love for God and for neighbor. The law of duty was consumed by the law and fire of love. Actions were no longer driven by fear but were inspired, fueled, and directed by the law of love.

It was this experience of God's love for him and an awakened love for God that firmly anchored Wesley's life in the spiritual disciplines that included acts of mercy and compassion as clearly as they included acts of piety and devotion.

Therefore it is not surprising that Wesley practiced and encouraged others to practice a way of life that expressed its faith in visible and real ways. Gathering for worship, prayer, song, study, witness, and confession gave energy to the incredible mission of the Methodists to the poor and marginalized of the day.

Where the Wesleyan movement is vital and actively engaged in mission today, we will find these same great streams of theology. We will find a deep and growing relationship to God that is nurtured by careful attention to and practice of the disciplines of the spiritual life. And out of this life of prayer and devotion flows a determined and unyielding commitment to God's people and their needs.

Today, as in every generation, there is the temptation to give attention to just one of these three great streams of theology. For some it is to revel in the love of God with little thought of what it means to love God in return. For others it is to be immersed in activity, convinced that we alone can save the world and need little help from God or others. Still others of us believe that if we pray, worship, tithe, and offer our love to God, we have done it all. And perhaps for all there is the temptation to forget that it is God who initiates our relationship. It is indeed amazing grace that calls us, sets us free, and sustains us day by day.

Wesleyans at their best, like their father in the Methodist faith, wed and hold together these three theological strands into one mighty stream of faith and works. When and where, by God's grace, we are able to weave these three strands together, there the Body of Christ is visible and active in the world. There people will see God at work, experience God's love, and find their love for God and neighbor awakened and strengthened. God's love and ours—a trustworthy pathway to faithful discipleship.

Spiritual Reading

And I know it also by St. John's plain rule, "If any man love the world, the love of the Father is not in him." For I love the world. I desire the things of the world, some or other of them, and have done all my life. I have always placed some part of my happiness in some or other of the things that are seen. Particularly in meat and drink, and in the company of those I loved. For many years, I have been, yea, and still am, hankering after a happiness, in loving, and being loved by one or another. And in these I have from time to time taken more pleasure than in God. *Journal, Vol. 1, p. 171*

John Merriman, a blind man, desires to return thanks to Almighty God, for the discovery of His love to him, an old sinner. *Journal, Vol. 1, p. 398*

In the morning I preached at Bentley-Wood-Green, on, "Be ye perfect, as your Father which is in heaven is perfect." Mr. G. afterwards told me, that this perfection he firmly believed and daily prayed for, namely, the love of God and man producing all those fruits which are described in our Lord's Sermon upon the mount. *Journal, Vol. 3, p. 67*

We are still "encompassed with a cloud of witnesses," who have testified, and do testify, in life and in death, that perfection which I have taught these forty years! This perfection cannot be a delusion, unless the Bible be a delusion too: I mean, "loving God with all our heart, and our neighbour as ourselves." I pin down all its opposers to this definition of it. No evasion! No shifting the question! Where is the delusion of this? Either you received this love, or you did not; if you did, dare you call it a delusion? You will not call it so for all the world. If you received any thing else, it does not at all affect the question. Be it as much a delusion as you please, it is nothing to them who have received quite another thing, namely, that deep communion with the Father and the Son, whereby they are enabled to give him their whole heart; to love every man as their own soul, and to walk as Christ also walked. *Journal, Vol. 3, p. 342*

But, supposing you had, do good designs and good desires make a Christian? By no means, unless they are brought to good effect. "Hell is paved," saith one, "with good intentions." The great question of all, then, still remains, Is the love of God shed abroad in your heart? Can you cry out, "My God, and my All?" Do you desire nothing but him? Are you happy in God? Is he your glory, your delight, your crown of rejoicing? And is this commandment written in your heart, "That he who loveth God love his brother also?" Do you then love your neighbour as yourself? Do you love every man, even your enemies, even the enemies of God, as your own soul? as Christ loved you? Yea, dost thou believe that Christ loved thee, and gave himself for thee? Hast thou faith in his blood? Believest thou the Lamb of God hath taken away thy sins, and cast them as a stone into the depth of the sea? that he hath blotted out the handwriting that was against thee, taking it out of the way, nailing it to his cross? Hast thou indeed redemption through his blood, even the remission of thy sins? And doth his Spirit bear witness with thy spirit, that thou art a child of God? *Sermon 2, The Almost Christian, Vol. 5, p. 24*

He that thus *loved* God, could not but love his brother also; and "not in word only, but in deed and in truth." "If God," said he, "so loved us, we ought also to love one another:" (1 John iv. 11;) yea, every soul of man, as "the mercy of God is over all his works." (Psalm cxlv. 9.) Agreeably hereto, the affection of this lover of God embraced all mankind for his sake; not excepting those whom he had never seen in the flesh, or those of whom he knew nothing more than that they were "the offspring of God," for whose souls his Son had died; not excepting the "evil" and "unthankful," and least of all his enemies, those who hated, or persecuted, or despitefully used him for his Master's sake. These had a peculiar place, both in his heart and in his prayers. He loved them "even as Christ loved us." *Sermon 4, Scriptural Christianity, Vol. 5, p. 40*

This seems not to be at all considered by those who so vehemently contend that a man must be sanctified, that is, holy, before he can be justified; especially by such of them as affirm, that universal holiness or obedience must precede justification. (Unless they mean that justification at the last day, which is wholly out of the present question.) So far from it, that the very supposition is not only flatly impossible, (for where there is no love of God, there is no holiness, and there is no love of God but from a sense of his loving us,) but also grossly, intrinsically absurd, contradictory to itself. For it is not a saint but a sinner that is forgiven, and under the notion of a sinner, God justifieth not the godly, but the ungodly; not those that are holy already, but the unholy. Upon what condition he doeth this, will be considered quickly: But whatever it is, it cannot be holiness. To assert this, is to say the Lamb of God takes away only those sins which were taken away before. *Sermon 5, Justification by Faith, Vol. 5, p. 58*

But on what terms, then, is he justified who is altogether *ungodly,* and till that time *worketh not?* On one alone; which is faith: He "believeth in Him that justifieth the ungodly." And "he that believeth is not condemned;" yea, he is "passed from death unto life." "For the righteousness (or mercy) of God is by faith of Jesus Christ unto all and upon all them that believe:—Whom God hath set forth for a propitiation, through faith in his blood; that he might be just, and" (consistently with his justice) "the Justifier of him which believeth in Jesus:" "Therefore we conclude that a man is justified by faith without the deeds of the law;" without previous obedience to the moral law, which, indeed, he could not, till now, perform. That it is the moral law, and that alone, which is here intended, appears evidently from the words that follow: "Do we then make void the law through faith? God forbid: Yea, we establish the law." What law do we establish by faith? Not the ritual law: Not the ceremonial law of Moses. In nowise; but the great, unchangeable law of love, the holy love of God and of our neighbour. *Sermon 5, Justification by Faith, Vol. 5, p. 60*

26

Going On to Perfection

❖— *Scripture Sentence*
But as for you ... pursue righteousness, godliness, faith, love, endurance, gentleness. Fight the good fight of the faith; take hold of the eternal life, to which you were called. *1 Timothy 6:11-12*

❖— *Scripture Readings*

1 Peter 3:8-12	*Matthew 5:43-48
2 Corinthians 2:12-17	Colossians 1:24-29
2 Corinthians 4:7-18	Matthew 7:13-20
1 John 2:1-6	

❖— *Silence for Meditation*

❖— *Spiritual Reading*

❖— *Recording of Insights and Commitments*

❖— *Prayers of Thanks, Intercession, Petition, and Praise*

❖— *Hymn Portion*
Enlarge, inflame, and fill my heart with boundless charity divine, so shall I all my strength exert, and love them with a zeal like thine, and lead them to thy open side, the sheep for whom the Shepherd died. *UMH #650*

❖— *Offering All of Life to God*

❖— *Closing Affirmation*
Going on to perfection is going on to life. This day I will choose life! *Rueben Job*

—— Reflections ——

Perfection was a dominant theme in John Wesley's preaching and practice. From the days at Oxford and the Holy Club until his death, he sought a way of living that would lead him closer to God. He wanted to be closer to God and he also wanted to be closer to God's plan and purpose for his life. For him the call to perfection was the call of God for everyone.

There was a strong yearning for perfection deep within his life and he responded to that yearning by a disciplined life aimed at loving God and neighbor all day every day of his life. Such a disciplined life was not burdensome, but liberating. It was not a morbid affair under an unbearable burden of guilt going on to a destructive self-examination and condemnation. Going on to perfection was a way of living that offered freedom, meaning, and joy. To be moving toward perfection was to be moving toward life at its best.

John Wesley believed that living the life of love of God and neighbor was to be on the road to perfection. And this road was not a dead-end road, but rather a pathway to life. To be moving toward this life of love was to be moving toward God. And moving toward God meant moving toward life in ever richer and more meaningful expressions.

For Wesley, Christian perfection was no more and no less than acceptance of the simple and profound truth of "Christ living in me." With Christ dwelling within, there could be no other road to follow than the road to perfection, the road to God. With Christ dwelling within, the impossible goal of perfection suddenly came within reach. For "it is no longer I who live, but it is Christ who lives in me" (Gal. 2:20). Once self has been moved from the center of life and that center is filled with Christ, Christian perfection does come within reach. Not because of our goodness, efforts, or merit, but because Christ dwelling within us provides both direction and power to travel this high road of loving God and neighbor. This is the road to perfection.

It is a road all are called to travel, and none is called to travel it alone. The thought of perfection, apart from the intervention of God in our lives, is at best terrifying. But with Christ dwelling within, giving direction, courage, and strength, the journey becomes not only bearable, but enormously challenging and deeply rewarding.

Life itself is a journey. From the moment of our birth until the moment of our death we are on the move. We are continually moving toward life or away from life. So, it is appropriate that we ask ourselves where it will all end if we keep on the road we now travel. Are we moving toward God or away from God? Does our daily journey lead us closer to God or farther from God? Are we on the road to perfection and life, or on the road to imperfection and death?

The truth is that we are not always on the same road. There are times when we do have our face turned toward God and desire only to love God and neighbor. And there are other times when we have turned away from God to focus on some distraction along the way. This is all a natural part of our faith journey and an experience that few escape. We should not be discouraged when we find ourselves in one of those moments of distraction. A better way to deal with these distractions is to recognize them and receive them as a sign of our need to turn towards God and the path toward perfection once more. The distraction can become a help as it calls us to awareness of our need of God and of God's readiness to fulfill that need and to walk with us in all of life.

Wesley believed that the opposition to Christian perfection grew out of misunderstanding rather than genuine resistance to the holy life. Those persons who are serious about their faith journey want no part of a false piety or an unrealistic expectation about how one can live. These persons want an authentic faith that grows out of and is nurtured by a vital relationship with the living God. And this is precisely what Christian perfection proposes to be.

Do you want to go on to perfection? If not, where do you want to go? The church and the world could be transformed if every person who claims Christ as Savior were to intentionally walk this road to perfection. May it always be the road for you.

——— *Spiritual Reading* ———

Perhaps the general prejudice against Christian perfection may chiefly arise from a misapprehension of the nature of it. We willingly allow, and continually declare, there is no such perfection in this life, as implies either a dispensation from doing good, and attending all the ordinances of God, or a freedom from ignorance, mistake, temptation, and a thousand infirmities necessarily connected with flesh and blood. *A Plain Account of Christian Perfection, Vol. 11, p. 383*

A year or two after, Mr. Law's "Christian Perfection" and "Serious Call" were put into my hands. These convinced me, more than ever, of the absolute impossibility of being half a Christian; and I determined, through his grace, (the absolute necessity of which I was deeply sensible of,) to be all-devoted to God, to give him all my soul, my body, and my substance. *A Plain Account of Christian Perfection, Vol. 11, p. 367*

All the difficulty is, to fix the meaning of it according to the word of God. And this we have done again and again, declaring to all the world, that Christian perfection does not imply an exemption from ignorance, or mistake, or infirmities, or temptations; but that it does imply the being so crucified with Christ, as to be able to testify, "I live not, but Christ liveth in me." (Gal. ii. 20.) and hath "purified my heart by faith." (Acts xv. 9.) It does not imply "the casting down every high thing that exalteth itself against the knowledge of God, and bringing into captivity every thought to the obedience of Christ." It does imply "the being holy, as he that hath called us is holy, in all manner of conversation:" (2 Cor. x. 5; 1 Peter i. 15;) and, in a word, "the loving the Lord our God with all our heart, and serving him with all our strength." *An Earnest Appeal to Men of Reason and Religion, Vol. 8, p. 22*

What is then the perfection of which man is capable while he dwells in a corruptible body? It is the complying with that kind command, "My son, give me thy heart." It is the "loving the Lord his God with all his heart, and with all his soul and with all his mind." This is the sum of Christian perfection: It is all comprised in that one word, Love. The first branch of it is the love of God: And as he that loves God loves his brother also, it is inseparably connected with the second: "Thou shalt love thy neighbour as thyself:" Thou shalt love every man as thy own soul, as Christ loved us. "On these two commandments hang all the Law and the Prophets:" These contain the whole of Christian perfection. *Sermon 76, On Perfection, Vol. 6, p. 413*

Christian perfection, therefore, does not imply (as some men seem to have imagined) an exemption either from ignorance, or mistake, or infirmities, or temptations. Indeed, it is only another term for holiness. They are two names for the same thing. Thus, every one that is holy is, in the Scripture sense, perfect. Yet we may, Lastly, observe, that neither in this respect is there any absolute perfection on earth. There is no *perfection of degrees*, as it is termed; none which does not admit of a continual increase. *Sermon 40, Christian Perfection, Vol. 6, p. 5*

By Christian Perfection, I mean, 1. Loving God with all our heart. Do you object to this? I mean, 2. A heart and life all devoted to God. Do you desire less? I mean, 3. Regaining the whole image of God. What objection to this? I mean, 4. Having all the mind that was in Christ. Is this going too far? I mean, 5. Walking uniformly as Christ walked. And this surely no Christian will object to. If any one means anything more, or anything else by Perfection, I have no concern with it. *Journal, Vol. 3, p. 369*

Monday, 30, and the two following days, I examined the society at Bristol, and was surprised to find fifty members fewer than I left in it last October. One reason is, Christian Perfection has been little insisted on; and wherever this is not done, be the Preachers ever so eloquent, there is little increase, either in the number or the grace of the hearers. *Journal, Vol. 3, p. 237*

In 1727 I read Mr. Law's "Christian Perfection," and "Serious Call," and more explicitly resolved to be all devoted to God, in body, soul, and spirit. In 1730 I began to be *homo unius libri;*(1) to study (comparatively) no book but the Bible. I then saw, in a stronger light than ever before, that only one thing is needful, even faith that worketh by the love of God and man, all inward and outward holiness; and I groaned to love God with all my heart, and to serve Him with all my strength. *Journal, Vol. 3, p. 213*

Removing soon after to another College, I executed a resolution which I was before convinced was of the utmost importance,—shaking off at once all my trifling acquaintance, I began to see more and more the value of time. I applied myself closer to study. I watched more carefully against actual sins: I advised others to be religious, according to that scheme of religion by which I modelled my own life. But meeting now with Mr. Law's "Christian Perfection" and "Serious Call," although I was much offended at many parts of both, yet they convinced me more than ever of the exceeding height and breadth and depth of the law of God. The light flowed in so mightily upon my soul, that every thing appeared in a new view. I cried to God for help, and resolved not to prolong the time of obeying Him as I had never done before. And by my continued endeavour to keep His whole law, inward and outward, to the utmost of my power, I was persuaded that I should be accepted of Him, and that I was even then in a state of salvation. *Journal, Vol. 1, p. 99*

What then was Christian perfection for Wesley? It was a perfection in love. "This is the sum of Christian perfection—loving God and loving our neighbor—these contain the whole of Christian perfection!" Wesley spoke of "inward holiness" (love of God and the assurance of God's love for us) and "outward holiness" (love of neighbor and deeds of kindness). Without ever implying sinless perfection, Wesley believed in a hope and expectation that our motives will be purified in love and thus move closer to the goal of perfect love God has for us.

Wesley was fond of speaking of persons being "happy and holy." For him the two experiences, far from being opposites, are actually one reality. "Why are you not happy?" Wesley frequently asked—only to answer, "Other circumstances may concur, but the main reason is because you are not holy."

Holiness always remains a gift of grace, not a merited achievement.

The arrogance and self-righteousness that characterized the "sanctification" and "second blessing" movements in America earlier in this century caused many persons in the Wesleyan heritage to, as Outler put it, throw the Wesleyan baby of true holiness out with the "second blessing" bathwater. This is unfortunate. Sanctification, if properly understood, is a rich doctrine full of deep spiritual potential for Christians and the church. Wesley took perfection to be "the grand depositum which God has lodged with the people called Methodists; and for the sake of propagating this chiefly He appeared to have raised us up." *Lovett Weems, Pocket Guide to John Wesley's Message Today, pp. 58–59*

*S*OURCES

The Book of Discipline of The United Methodist Church 1996. Nashville: The United Methodist Publishing House, 1996.

Harper, Steve. *Devotional Life in the Wesleyan Tradition.* Nashville: Upper Room Books, 1983.

Heitzenrater, Richard P. *Wesley and the People Called Methodists.* Nashville: Abingdon Press, 1995.

Jackson, Thomas, editor. *The Works of John Wesley on Compact Disc.* Franklin, TN: Providence House Publishers, 1995.

Jennings, Theodore W., Jr. *Good News to the Poor.* Nashville: Kingswood Books, 1990.

Kimbrough, ST and Beckerlegge, Oliver A., editors. *The Unpublished Poetry of Charles Wesley.* Volume II. Nashville: Kingswood Books, 1990.

Langford, Thomas A. *Practical Divinity.* Nashville: Abingdon Press, 1983.

Maddox, Randy L. *Responsible Grace: John Wesley's Practical Theology.* Nashville: Kingswood Books, 1994.

Marquardt, Manfred. *John Wesley's Social Ethics.* Nashville: Abingdon Press, 1992.

Mulholland, M. Robert. *Shaped by the Word.* Nashville: Upper Room Books, 1985.

Rack, Henry D. *Reasonable Enthusiast.* Nashville: Abingdon Press, 1992.

Taylor, Blaine. *John Wesley: A Blueprint for Church Renewal.* Champaign, IL: C-4 Resources, 1984.

The United Methodist Hymnal. Nashville: The United Methodist Publishing House, 1996.

Weems, Lovett H. *Pocket Guide to John Wesley's Message Today.* Nashville: Abingdon Press, 1991.

SCRIPTURE INDEX

The Scripture Sentences, Scripture Readings, and scriptural Closing Affirmations are indexed here. The scripture passages identified as primary texts for each of the twenty-six themes are identified with an asterisk (*).